THE
REPUBLICAN DREAM TEAM OF 2016

A Strategy for Republicans to Win

CATHERINE S. McBREEN
KATHY SEEI

RIVER GROVE
BOOKS

Published by River Grove Books
Austin, TX
www.rivergrovebooks.com

Copyright ©2016 Catherine S. McBreen and Kathleen Seei

All rights reserved.

No part of this book may be reproduced, stored in a retrieval system, or transmitted by any means, electronic, mechanical, photocopying, recording, or otherwise, without written permission from the copyright holder.

Distributed by River Grove Books

Design and composition by Greenleaf Book Group and Sheila Parr
Cover design by Greenleaf Book Group and Sheila Parr
Cover images: © Shutterstock / David Evison, Fedele Ferrara

Cataloging-in-Publication data is available.

Print ISBN: 978-1-63299-080-8

eBook ISBN: 978-1-63299-081-5

First Edition

This book is dedicated to:

The Republican Dream Team of 2016. As we finish writing you are in the heat of the primary race, refining your positions on issues and coming together to defy the biased media. We have never before witnessed such a large, talented group of candidates. You inspired us to write this book. We hope you will read it and take to heart the possibilities of our ideas.

The Voters. You will be selecting the Republican nominee and the President of the United States of America in 2016. Thank you for paying attention to your civic duty. As we write the book you are breaking all records for viewership of the Republican Presidential Debates. We hope our book will provide you a way to stay engaged and turn out to vote . . . even if your preferred Republican candidate does not win the primary.

Our Husbands, Children and Grandchildren who have supported us as we worked to get this book into the hands of readers before the first Republican Primary.

Our Forefathers who drafted our constitution and who continue to inspire us to keep their audacious idea alive and well into the future. . .

"WE THE PEOPLE of the United States, in Order to form a more perfect Union, establish Justice, insure domestic Tranquility, provide for the common defence, promote the general Welfare, and secure the Blessings of Liberty to ourselves and our Posterity, do ordain and establish the Constitution for the United States of America"

CONTENTS

Foreword ix

Chapter 1: The Republican Dream Team Concept 1

Chapter 2: What Do Voters Really Worry About? 9

Chapter 3: The Roles of the President,
Vice President and Cabinet 15

Chapter 4: The Traits Voters are Seeking
in a Candidate 33

Chapter 5: The Businessman/Woman
and the Professional 41

Chapter 6: The Governors 49

Chapter 7: The Senators 59

Chapter 8: The Voters Identify their Issues 67

Chapter 9: The Voters Rank the Candidates 77

Chapter 10: The Candidates and the Issues 93

Chapter 11: Voters and the Dream Team Concept 129

Chapter 12: The Influencers 135

Chapter 13: Republican Dream Team 2016
Takes the Stage 141

Chapter 14: What's at Stake? 151

Appendix A: The Dream Team Pledge 157

Appendix B: Voter Worksheet 159

Appendix C: Overview of Candidates 161

FOREWORD

The idea of a Republican "Dream Team" started as many great ideas start, with two thoughtful people intensely discussing an issue over a glass of wine. At the family reunion June of 2015, Catherine McBreen and her aunt, Kathy Seei, were musing about one of their favorite topics-politics and the upcoming 2016 Presidential election and their desire for the Republicans to win the White House. They began to formulate a "what if" scenario to solve the problem of a highly qualified, albeit over-crowed, field of candidates running for the ticket's top spot. Thus was born the concept for the book *The Republican Dream Team of 2016*.

Our forefathers wrote our Constitution in future perfect language. Their intent was to document and codify the fundamental rights and obligations of a free nation. They used the limited communication tools available to them to present the duties of a limited federal government to the first citizens of the United States of America. They laid out a simple template for the organization of the national government with the necessary checks and balances built in through the three branches: executive, legislative and judicial. They were silent on the organizational structure that extends below those basic branches. One can only imagine if they were here today what they would think about how much "extends below" that structure today.

> "In the 2012 presidential election only 57.5 percent of eligible voters turned out. That is sobering. Even worse is having to go back to 1896 to find a rate significantly higher (79 percent)" —Tom Taft, Editorial, Dallas Morning News, November 9, 2015

Large federal government structures bind American prosperity with numerous regulations, managed by larger silos of employees funded by picking the pockets of American families and businesses. The result is a government increasingly unable to maintain the United States' standing as a competitive nation and a world leader. In contrast, corporations reinvent themselves, merge and do whatever it takes to survive in the ever-changing environment in which they find themselves-or they cease to exist. When government survives the national debt increases, special interests are pandered to in order to win votes and the average citizen looks at the vitriolic discourse and disengages.

As authors we are concerned with what we see. Our Executive Branch is seeking to make changes without the restraining balance of the legislative branch. Our legislative bodies focus on power plays "to win" on individual points so specific constituencies can mark a special interest check sheet. As a result, the work of government is actually implemented by the very people who benefit from growing government-the non-elected bureaucrats. All the while our judicial branch meanders into issues best left to the discretion of states. Our goal is to begin a thoughtful national dialogue backed by research on what citizens are thinking and an idea that could win the 2016 Presidential election and jump start the reform of our national government.

While reading this book you may feel that you are hearing two very distinct voices and in fact you are. One is the voice of a recovering politician who came of age during the 1960s and spent her life chasing innovation in both the public and private sectors. The other is 20 years younger with the more measured voice of a trained lawyer who explores the future from the studied view of data. It is our hope that the conclusions drawn in this book meet somewhere in the middle.

The information provided in the charts included in this book comes from a variety of information sources readily available on the candidates' campaign websites and Wikipedia. The goal is to bring all of the information and differing as well as similar views together in one place where you, the reader and the voter, can easily assess it. All candidates have been forwarded the information contained in this book with our publication date and a request for them to edit what we have collected. Should additional information become available after the book is published, all corrections will be posted on The Republican Dream Team of 2016 website. We hope you will use The Republican Dream Team of 2016 as a Voters' Guide. We have included a guided process in Appendix B for this purpose. Please join us in our pursuit of these ideas in the following ways:

Website: www.republicandreamteamof2016
Twitter: @rdtbook
Facebook: www.facebook.com/Republican-Dream-Team-of-2016

CHAPTER 1

THE REPUBLICAN DREAM TEAM CONCEPT

The 24/7-news cycle has forced the 2016 Presidential election into the forefront of the media coverage months before even the first primary or straw poll occurs. Seventeen Republicans initially announced their candidacy for President, creating enormous confusion for potential voters and considerable fodder for discussion by the talking heads of the cable news channels. (As of November 2015 that number has been reduced to 14.) As for the Democrats, their coronation of Hillary Clinton changed from relatively uneventful to slightly more precarious as she fights off attacks regarding her email server choices as well as a more-popular-than-expected Bernie Sanders. Hillary's coronation, although probable, is no longer guaranteed.

Voters are paying attention to the Presidential election of 2016. In the fall of 2015, Spectrem Group, a highly respected consulting and research firm tested the concept of a slate of candidates both quantitatively and qualitatively with potential voters. Over 500 individuals likely to vote in the Presidential primaries completed an online survey in November 2015. Additionally, a focus group was held with Republican and Independent voters (10 individuals) in October 2015. This research will be discussed throughout this book and will hereinafter be referred to as "The Research".

In The Research, 43 percent of voters indicated that they are "very informed" about the 2016 Presidential election and 47 percent said they were "somewhat informed". Only 10 percent indicated they knew little about the election. Older voters were the most likely to indicate they are "very informed".

Additionally, 36 percent of the respondents had watched both of the Republican debates that occurred prior to the onset of the survey fielding and 27 percent had watched at least one of the debates. Once again, older voters were the most likely to have watched both debates.

Republican voters are hopeful. When asked their opinion of potential candidates, individuals polled during general lunchtime or meeting conversations respond as follows:

"I don't really know. I kind of like a lot of them."

"There are so many. But any of them would be better than what we have now."

"I think they should work together . . . not against each other. They all have different strengths and weaknesses."

The vast field of candidates intrigues voters. Whether it's the fresh face of the young Marco Rubio, the safe feeling of an establishment candidate such as Jeb Bush, the candor of a Chris Christie, or the business success of a Carly Fiorina, each of these candidates has some appeal to Republican voters. Although Scott Walker is no longer in the race, he has the folkloric appeal of taking on the Unions, while Dr. Ben Carson, the intellectual and an African American, represents the ultimate American success story. John Kasich, Lindsey Graham, Ted Cruz, Rand Paul . . . each has a different message and a core support system. And, of course, there is Donald Trump, the bombastic entrepreneur who is out to convince everyone that he could be "a really good President."

In fact, a third of the voters who responded to The Research felt that the quality of the candidates running exceeds that of the candidates that have run in previous elections. This is especially true for those over age 65 at 41 percent. Forty-three percent indicate that the quality of the candidates is similar to previous elections.

Traditionally, a Presidential candidate is chosen based upon the outcome of the primaries. As the primary season progresses, various candidates begin to withdraw from the race, generally due to the fact that they aren't appealing to enough voters and they need additional funding to pay for the expensive advertising campaigns required to run for President. In the 2012 elections, it is estimated that the Republicans spent $1,141,214,942 (www.OpenSecrets blog.com). In that election, 11 candidates were involved in the run up to the primaries with only three candidates staying in the race until the end. And as everyone knows, Mitt Romney was chosen to represent the Republicans and ultimately lost to the incumbent, President Barack Obama.

The candidate is ultimately chosen based upon a whittling down of the primary field and the aggregation of enough electoral votes from various states to ensure that the candidate will receive the required votes at the

Republican convention. Prior to the convention, the projected candidate will choose a running mate. In most cases, the running mate will be an individual that the candidate and the Party feel will attract additional voters because of some particular characteristic. For example, John McCain chose Alaskan Governor Sarah Palin in the 2008 elections perhaps to appeal to women voters. Palin was also the parent of a special needs child. In 2012, Mitt Romney chose young, articulate House Representative Paul Ryan who was perceived to be tough on the budget deficit and was from a swing state, Wisconsin.

The last time a candidate chose an individual who was a competitor during the primaries was in 1980 when Ronald Reagan chose George H.W. Bush. Therefore, it is perceived as unlikely that any of the 17 original candidates vying for President in 2016 could be chosen as Vice President. Considering, however, how Ronald Reagan has entered icon status within the Republican Party, maybe his approach should be reconsidered. Many of these individuals, who have great ideas on how to approach foreign policy or how to change Obamacare to make it really work, are likely to fade into the landscape or eventually become pundits of some type. (Of course, those who are currently in the Senate or are currently acting as Governors will probably retain their posts.) But these individuals have great resumes, a love for their country, and for many being part of the team would be acceptable. It could also increase their name recognition and put them into a position to be considered as a candidate in the next Presidential election.

But what if, instead of dissing the rest of the field, a candidate or the collective Republican Party was smart or brave enough to actually present the populace with a slate of an administration, not just a President and Vice President? What if some of the primary competitors were listed as the potential Secretary of State, Secretary of Health and Human Services, Secretary of Defense, as well as guaranteed other Cabinet positions or posts within the administration? Would that be appealing to voters? Would providing voters with a team of qualified individuals, rather than just a President and Vice Presidential candidates make a difference? What if the Republicans ran a Dream Team in 2016? (Note that Donald Trump tweeted Carl Icahn, a highly respected businessman, and asked if he would be his Secretary of Treasury in August of 2015. Icahn tweeted back his acceptance.)

In 1989, the Olympic rules were changed to allow professional basketball players to compete in the Summer Olympics. Prior to that time, the U.S. sometimes struggled in the basketball competition despite the fact that the NBA is by far the most competitive league internationally. In 1988, the U.S. won the bronze medal. Those countries that did not have professional basketball as a sport, such as the then existing USSR, were able to compete with individuals that were not "professionals" despite the fact that the Russian athletes spent the largest percentage of their time preparing for the Olympics. In 1992, the U.S. was first able to take advantage of this rule and they brought together the best players in the NBA, including Michael Jordan, Magic Johnson, Larry Bird, Scottie Pippen and others. In fact, 10 of the 12 players on this team have been named to the NBA's official list of the 50 greatest players of the league's first 50 years. This team easily brought home the gold medal to the U.S. and was known as the Dream Team.

Is it time for a Dream Team to be created in the political

landscape? Would voters of all types be more energized to support a slate of candidates that includes a number of individuals that held various types of competencies?

Of course, it is impossible to elect a slate of candidates in the current system. Voters are only allowed to vote for the President and Vice President. But, what if the Presidential and Vice Presidential candidates made a "handshake" promise to voters that they would appoint some of their primary competitors as well as maybe other highly regarded Republicans to their Cabinet?

For example, despite who becomes the Presidential candidate, which is impossible to predict at this particular point, what if those candidates who have specific skills could be considered for certain spots, such as:

- *Secretary of Treasury* . . . perhaps a business person such as Donald Trump or Carly Fiorina?
- *Secretary of State* . . . perhaps Lindsey Graham who has been on the Senate Foreign Relations Committee or Rick Perry who as Governor of Texas has dealt with the issue of illegal aliens crossing the border or Marco Rubio who has worked with members of Congress already to try to solve the immigration crisis?
- *Attorney General* . . . maybe Governor Chris Christie who was formerly a prosecutor in New Jersey?

These opportunities will be explored in the next few chapters. We will highlight the experience of the candidates and their stands on issues of importance to Republican voters. The Dream Team concept and whether it will be acceptable or attractive to voters has also been tested.

To effectively analyze the candidates throughout this book, the candidates have been broken into the following groups:

Governors	Senators	Business and Professionals
Jeb Bush	Ted Cruz	Ben Carson
Chris Christie	Lindsey Graham	Carly Fiorina
Jim Gilmore	Rand Paul	Donald Trump
Mike Huckabee	Marco Rubio	
John Kasich	Rick Santorum	
George Pataki		

The candidates that have already dropped out of the race (Scott Walker, Bobby Jindal, and Rick Perry) have been included in some of the analysis, primarily because they may have skills that would contribute to the Republican Dream Team concept.

Why did we separate the candidates into groups? Governors have expressed the viewpoint that they have been "executives" and know how to run a government and actually get things accomplished. The Senators, however, claim they know the needs and desires of their electorates, the in-depth issues regarding specific federal issues, and how to get things approved in Congress. In contrast, the so-called outsider candidates from the business world argue that career politicians don't get things done and that they bring a fresh approach to solving the nation's problems.

By analyzing the strengths and weaknesses of the 14 remaining candidates, as well as some of the perceptions of those who have already dropped out, and comparing them to the opinions of actual voters, perhaps the Republicans can build a "Dream Team" that can not only win the 2016 Presidential election but can work as a team to make necessary system improvements to the executive branch of our government.

The margin of error is 4 percent. Keep in mind that this research is not political polling and was meant to capture more of the underlying attitudes of voters about specific issues than polling generally is able to uncover. Also, the research was conducted at a point in time, November of 2015, and is subject to the multiple events that will occur prior to the elections. This research is not meant to be predictive of election outcomes but rather is meant to explore various concepts. In some chapters, additional Spectrem research will be referred to and will be identified at that time.

This exploration of the Republican Dream Team concept provides a new and different way to approach the Republican primaries, plan for winning the general election and jump start the transformation of the Executive branch of government.

CHAPTER 2

WHAT DO VOTERS REALLY WORRY ABOUT?

Voters today are worried about numerous issues but ultimately national security, the economy and how these issues impact their lives is the greatest concern for most households. Voters believe that government has an enormous impact on the economy and the inability of government to work effectively has been a consistent concern of these households since the onset of the financial crisis in 2007. Of course, any threat to our national security not only impacts our peace of mind but also impacts the economy should an attack occur on U.S. soil—as does the consideration of adding more immigrants to an already weak job environment.

Every month since 2004, more than 500 households with more than $50,000 of net worth (not including the value of their primary residence) have been surveyed by Spectrem Group and asked what they are worried about. All of the research cited in this chapter is based upon Spectrem's ongoing monthly research and is not part of The Research conducted for this book. The sample discussed in this chapter represents the views of more than 6,000 households. The margin of error for the research is around 3 percent. Findings reflect the following:

- Since 2009 respondents have rated the Political Environment as their top national concern. In the summer of 2015, 82 percent of individuals identified the Political Environment as their top national concern followed by Government Gridlock at 78 percent.
- Three quarters of households surveyed worry about tax increases, 72 percent fear terrorism and 71 percent are worried about the National Debt.

These are issues over which voters have little control. While some topic areas peaked upward at certain times, driven primarily by media coverage of specific events, for the most part concern about these issues has remained steady. Note that voter worries about tax increases climbed in 2012 when Congress was working to avoid having the U.S. fall off the fiscal cliff. The Government Gridlock worries actually decreased slightly in late 2014 when Congress was taken over by one party . . . but subsequent veto challenges by President Obama made Government Gridlock float back into the Top 5 Concerns once again.

It should be noted that the sixth Top National Concern is Stock Market Performance, which concerns 70 percent of households. Volatility due to global economic issues can quickly move this issue to the top of the list, as it did for a short while in September of 2015.

National Concerns are only important because they ultimately impact the Personal Concerns that voters worry about in their everyday lives. These Personal Concerns can easily be lumped into one large category . . . caring for themselves and their loved ones. There are three large categories that consistently jump out in the research that Spectrem Group has conducted in the past two decades. It boils down to Health Issues, Retirement, and Maintaining my Financial Position.

Let's discuss Health issues first. Fifty-four percent of individuals worry about their own health. While there is some variation in percentages based upon age, roughly half of those under 35 worry about their health while the number increases to about 60 percent for those over age 65. It's interesting to note, however, that 63 percent of individuals worry about the health of their spouse. This is a higher percentage than those who are worried about their own health! These percentages increase as age increases.

Related to health issues is the challenges individuals face when dealing with catastrophic health events. With the aging of the population, there are greater worries about spending one's final years in a care facility and the financial impact that may have on one's family. Fifty-four percent of households worry about ending up in a nursing home while forty-eight percent of households worry about caring for and supporting aging parents. (This is particularly true of households currently between the ages of 44-65.) As individuals live longer, they may face many years of health issues and place even greater pressure on the "sandwich generation".

Sixty two percent of households are worried about being able to retire when they want. While this percentage has decreased since the height of the financial crisis, it remains important to almost two-thirds of the population. While individuals under age 35 register at 31 percent regarding their retirement concerns, households over the age of 36 have significant retirement worries with 67 percent of individuals between the ages of 45 and 54 being worried about being able to retire when they want.

Clearly being able to fund one's retirement and ensure that a family or individual does not run out of money too early is the ultimate retirement concern. Forty-three percent of voters worry about depleting their retirement funds. The primary reason? Seventy percent are worried about the cost of healthcare during their retirement years. Forty three percent worry about Taxes and 37 percent simply worry about spending too much.

Finally, 60 percent of voters worry about Maintaining Their Financial Position. For those who are still working, this may mean ensuring they don't lose their job. It also means helping their children out as needed (52 percent worry about their children's financial position.) For those who are already retired, it means being able to depend on their income stream, regardless of where it may come from. Retirees are also worried about their cost of living remaining the same, thus rising gas or food prices are seen as threats.

While these three items-Health Issues, Retirement, and Maintaining One's Financial Position-are what matters to voters, we hear few of these issues being addressed on a day-to-day basis. Instead, the news media spends significant amounts of time on issues such as Caitlyn Jenner's transition, climate change and the "Deflategate" controversy.

In June of 2015, voters were asked to identify from a long list of current event items what they identified as the most important Current Event. Note that later in this book, additional research will be discussed that was completed in November of 2015 ("The Research"). The Research is discussed further in Chapter 8. In June of 2015, 38 percent of individuals chose ISIS and terrorist threats as their greatest concern. Fifty percent of Republican voters chose this topic as the most important at that time, as did 38 percent of Independent voters. Only 21 percent of Democrats identified ISIS as the most important Current Event.

In contrast, 35 percent of Democrats identified Climate Change as the most important Current Event. This compares to only 17 percent of the total along with seventeen percent of Independents identified and only 5 percent of Republicans who feel similarly.

Sixteen percent of voters listed Computer Hacking threats as the Current Event they felt was most important in June of 2015. Race Relations and Police Brutality weighed in at 11 percent and 5 percent respectively. When the survey was fielded in June, Vladimir Putin was important to 4 percent of voters. Pulling troops out of the Middle East ranked with 7 percent. Caitlyn Jenner, Tom Brady and the FIFA scandal all weighed in at 1 percent.

While LGBT issues and race relations are important and interesting to discuss on cable news, these are not the issues that voters are likely to rely upon when choosing the next President. Ultimately, the candidate that they believe can most effectively control and overcome their concerns about the political climate and government gridlock will win their support.

CHAPTER 3

THE ROLES OF THE PRESIDENT, VICE PRESIDENT AND CABINET

Remember the U.S. Government course that you took in high school? Most of us don't. Therefore a brief government lesson is in order. We will look briefly at the role of the President and the Vice President. But most importantly, the role of the Cabinet will be reviewed. This is probably one of the areas of government that we quickly overlook or forget about. But these individuals play an important role in the success of various governmental programs. Perhaps staffing these roles with competent individuals (as opposed to mere political appointees) may actually make government work more effectively.

A prime example of the need for competency when initiating a government plan is the rollout of Obamacare. Kathleen Sibelius was the Health and Human Services Secretary when the Affordable Care Act was implemented. Sibelius entered the Cabinet in 2009 as a highly regarded former governor of Kansas. While clearly Ms. Sibelius had management and executive experience, it is unlikely that in her former role as governor she was required to deal with the strategic and technological type of project planning required to effectively implement such an overwhelming and ill-defined program. In this particular case, someone with an extensive business strategy and operational background may have been more suited. Link this with an executive . . . the President . . . with no business background and it becomes inevitable that this project would be botched. If a bank or insurance company had been putting together this type of project plan, one could be certain that the implementation timeframe would have been extended by many years and enormous amounts of testing would have been required. Businesses, unlike the government, need to be certain that they are carefully and competently dealing with the private information of individuals. Therefore, someone with experience in large project planning and management may have been a better choice at that particular time. Instead, the President appointed a political appointee and achieved his goal of having a specific number of women in his Cabinet.

Thus, the idea that a Cabinet made up of competent, highly respected individuals identified prior to an election might make the electorate feel that government could work more effectively. Everyone knows that a President has too many responsibilities to oversee the day-to-day issues that arise in every part of government. Knowing that a strong leadership team was in place might overcome the concerns regarding government gridlock.

The Role of the President

Let's focus on the role of the President. Article II of the U.S. Constitution creates the executive branch of the government. Section 1, Clause 1 gives the President the

"Executive Power" of the government. The President has the power to appoint the Cabinet members as well as federal judges. The Senate, however, must approve all of these. Section 2, Clause 1 of the Constitution identifies the President as the Commander in Chief of the Army and Navy. He cannot, however, declare war. The President also has the power under Section 2, Clause 2 to make Treaties "by and with the Consent of the Senate".

The President can recommend to Congress "such measures as he shall judge necessary and expedient". Article II, Section 3, Clause 2 of the Constitution is known as the "Recommendation Clause" and is responsible for most of the initiatives a President puts forth in his or her agenda. Clause 4 requires the President to receive all "foreign Ambassadors" and Clause 5 makes the President responsible to "take care that the laws be faithfully executed". Multiple Supreme Court cases have interpreted this clause and ultimately require the President to enforce the laws, whether or not he agrees with them. Of course, over the years it has become clear that while the President must enforce a law, he sometimes can have a wide interpretation of how a particular law is defined. Thus the role of the Attorney General can be very important when a President is executing this particular power.

These powers, along with the power to commission military and Foreign Service officers, are clearly outlined in the U.S. Constitution. How these powers are interpreted is one of the hot topics that separate not only the political parties from each other, but sometimes different factions within each party. Because of the broad manner in which these powers may or may not be applied, the Cabinet becomes incredibly important in implementing various policies and procedures.

The Role of the Vice President

Once again, a history lesson is in order. According to *Wikipedia* and multiple other sources (as well as the author's own long forgotten high school history classes), the original intent of the Founders of the country was that the Vice President would be the candidate who received the second highest number of votes. When Thomas Jefferson and Aaron Burr were running for President, they tied. After numerous votes, Jefferson finally won, but was saddled with a Vice President he didn't really like. Since the Constitution states that the Vice President is the second in line for the Presidency . . . and should something happen to the President, the Vice President takes over . . . well, that could result in all kinds of nasty potential coincidences. The Twelfth Amendment took care of this problem by creating the party structure that exists today where a President and Vice President run together. It also gives the Vice President the responsibility of presiding over the counting of the votes for the Electoral College.

Article I, Section II of the U.S. Constitution, which discusses the powers of the President and Vice President, only outlines the fact that the Vice President is the second in line to the Presidency. There are no other powers identified for the Vice President in the executive branch of government. The Vice President is also the President of the Senate in accordance with Article I, Section 3, Clause 4 of the U.S. Constitution. In cases in which there may be a tie vote, the Vice President is responsible for casting the deciding vote. In recent years, the Vice President primarily performs a social or ambassadorial role, appearing at the funerals and other events of foreign leaders as well as key supporters within the U.S. The 25th Amendment to the

U.S. Constitution identifies how the role of the Vice President will be filled should the office become empty.

In recent elections, the Presidential nominee announces the candidate for the Vice-Presidency after their own nomination becomes fairly certain (i.e. he or she has won the required number of electoral votes in the primaries), but generally just before the party's convention. (The Vice Presidential candidate is formally approved at the convention.) The Republican Dream Team concept believes that the selection of the Vice-Presidential candidate is important to ensuring that the Republican Party is including the interests of multiple beliefs and voters within the Republican Party. With that in mind, the ability of a candidate to identify a potential running mate ... even one he or she may be running against ... would be beneficial in building support among voters.

In The Research conducted for this book, voters were asked how important the selection of the Vice-Presidential candidate is to obtaining their ultimate vote. Sixty-four percent of voters indicated that the Vice-Presidential selection is important or very important to them. Younger voters, those between the ages of 18–44, were less concerned about the Vice-Presidential candidate with only 53 percent indicating that they cared about the selection of the VP. If two or more candidates were able to combine forces at an earlier date, it might potentially build support for that combination of candidates among the voters.

The Role of the Cabinet

The Cabinet is not established under the Constitution or any of its amendments. Article II, Section 2 of the Constitution allows the President to appoint "Public Ministers and Consul". The Constitution also refers to "heads of departments" in Article II, Section 2, Clause 2. The Cabinet generally meets on a weekly basis and provides recommendations and advice to the President. In the United States Code, 5 USC Section 101, the Executive Departments are listed. This has been amended over the years changing the number of Cabinet members several times.

The White House website www.whitehouse.gov describes the Cabinet as follows:

> "The Cabinet is an advisory body made up of the heads of the 15 executive departments. Appointed by the President and confirmed by the Senate, the members of the Cabinet are often the President's closest confidants. In addition to running major federal agencies, they play an important role in the Presidential line of succession — after the Vice President, Speaker of the House, and Senate President pro tempore, the line of succession continues with the Cabinet offices in the order in which the departments were created. All the members of the Cabinet take the title Secretary, excepting the head of the Justice Department, who is styled Attorney General."

The 15 Cabinet members and the Vice-President attend the Cabinet meetings which are called by the President. (Note: the Vice-President was not invited to Cabinet meetings until 1919, according to Harold C. Relyea, *The Vice President: Evolution of the Modern Office 1933–2001*)

```
                    ┌─────────────────┐
                    │   PRESIDENT     │
                    └────────┬────────┘
                             │
                             │    ┌─────────────────┐
                             ├────│ VICE PRESIDENT  │
                             │    └─────────────────┘
        ┌────────────────────┴────────────────────┐
```

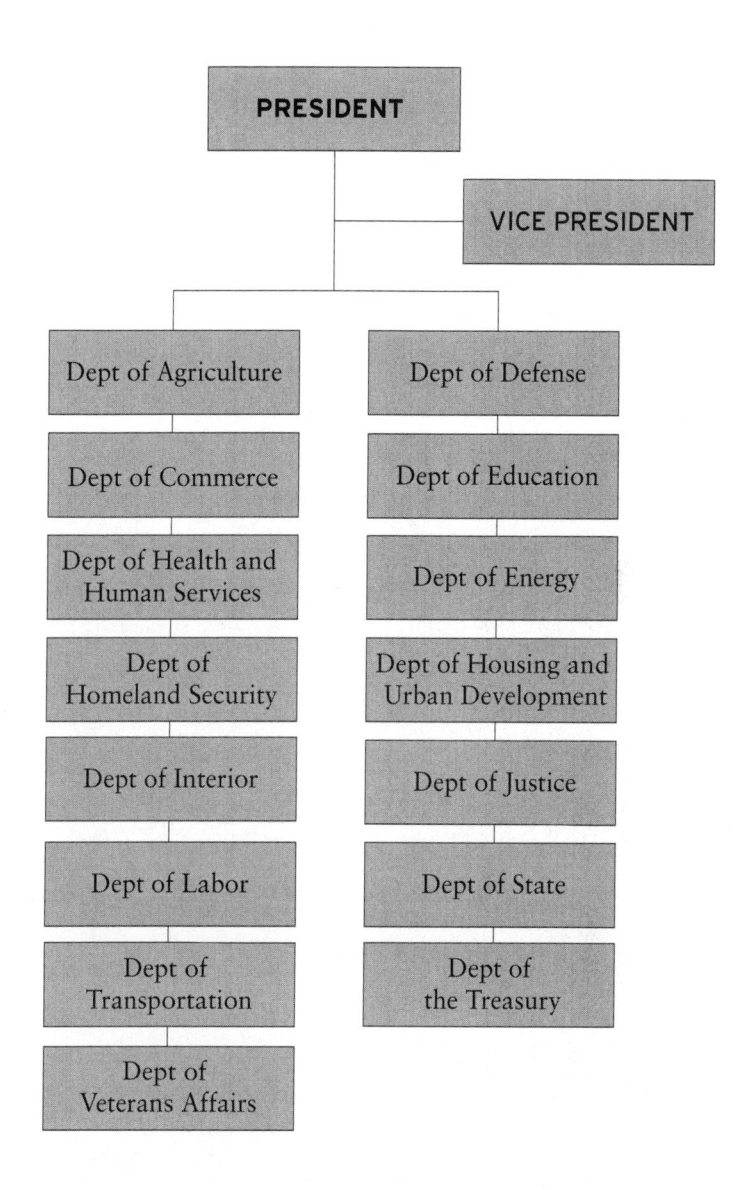

Dept of Agriculture	Dept of Defense
Dept of Commerce	Dept of Education
Dept of Health and Human Services	Dept of Energy
Dept of Homeland Security	Dept of Housing and Urban Development
Dept of Interior	Dept of Justice
Dept of Labor	Dept of State
Dept of Transportation	Dept of the Treasury
Dept of Veterans Affairs	

Seeking information on the responsibilities and targeted goals for each Cabinet post can be daunting. Each Cabinet post has its own website, none of which are consistent in format or types of information shared. The White House website provided the most consistent information on the duties and responsibilities of the individual Cabinet posts. Additional information for this book was obtained from the actual government websites for the department or agency. The "Issues" column provided in the following Recap is based on multiple media sources.

RECAP OF THE CABINET

The following is an overview of the size of each of the various executive departments. A Cabinet member oversees each of these departments and is generally known as the "Secretary of . . . .". For example, the leader of the Department of Defense is the Secretary of Defense. The only exception is the office of the Attorney General, who heads the Department of Justice. Needless to say, each Department consists of multiple agencies. The Size and Budget columns are based upon the information provided by www.whitehouse.gov and the "Key Challenges" column consists of issues identified by the authors.

	SIZE	BUDGET	DUTIES	KEY CHALLENGES
DEPT OF DEFENSE	1.3 million active military 700,000 civilians 1.1 million National Guard and reserves	$1.2 trillion	Provide military forces needed to deter war and protect the security of our country	ISIS America's role in the world
DEPT OF AGRICULTURE	100,000 employees	$95 billion	Executes farming, agriculture and food policy Administers to needs of farmers and ranchers Trade of agriculture internationally Food safety Ending hunger in U.S. Administers overseas aid	Reducing the number of Americans on SNAP (food stamp program) Determining when aid should be given to countries not supportive of U.S. Ensuring fair pricing of farm exports Impact of drought in California Genetically engineered crops

Continued

24 The Republican Dream Team of 2016

	SIZE	BUDGET	DUTIES	KEY CHALLENGES
DEPT OF THE TREASURY	100,000 employees	$13 billion	Ensuring economic prosperity and soundness of U.S. financial system Creates coins and currency Collects taxes Borrows funds Regulates banks and securities industry	Tax rates Scandals including improper segmenting of the IRS of conservative organizations Loss of emails in investigations such as the Lois Lerner investigation Determination of when and how much to raise interest rates Ongoing compliance and regulations regarding banks and other financial institutions National Debt

	SIZE	BUDGET	DUTIES	KEY CHALLENGES
DEPT OF JUSTICE	800,000 employees	$25 billion	Enforce laws and defend interests of US Ensure public safety against foreign and domestic threats Prevent and control crime Ensure fair and impartial administration of justice Includes FBI, DEA, US Marshalls and Federal Bureau of Prisons	Guantanamo Border safety Black Lives Matter debate Terrorism Deportation Immigration Review
DEPT OF EDUCATION	4,200 employees	$68.6 billion	Promote standards and achievement in education system Foster educational excellence Administer financial aid Collect data on schools	College loan debt and collections Comparison of U.S. schools to international competitors Re-examination of financial aid system Common Core

Continued

	SIZE	BUDGET	DUTIES	KEY CHALLENGES
DEPT OF ENERGY	100,000 employees	$23 billion	Advance national economic and energy security Develop clean and affordable energy Nuclear security Oversight of development of natural resources	Re-establishment of potential pipelines post Keystone pipeline event Oil in Arctic Circle and Russian attempts to develop Impact of climate change and related regulation New sources of energy
DEPT OF STATE	30,000 employees	$35 billion	Develops and implements foreign policy Immigration Diplomatic relations with more than 180 countries	Immigration policies Ongoing investigation of Benghazi Iran policy and nuclear deal Relationship with Israel Relationship with Russia, China as well as Allies
DEPT OF VETERANS AFFAIRS	235,000 employees	$90 billion	Administers benefits for veterans, families and survivors	VA hospitals accused recently of not effectively servicing vets

	SIZE	BUDGET	DUTIES	KEY CHALLENGES
DEPT OF TRANS- PORTATION	55,000 employees	$70 billion	Ensures safe, accessible and convenient transportation system Includes FAA, Federal Highway Admin, National Highway Traffic Safety Admin and Federal Railroad and Maritime Admin	Ensuring transportation system is safe from terrorist threats Developing rules for autos and other transportation to become environmentally efficient Impact of oil and gas prices
DEPT OF LABOR	15,000 employees	$50 billion	Ensures strong workforce Job training, safe working conditions, minimum wage, employment discrimination, and unemployment	Minimum wage debate Changing role and impact of unions

Continued

	SIZE	BUDGET	DUTIES	KEY CHALLENGES
DEPT OF THE INTERIOR	70,000 employees	$16 billion	Principal conservation agency Protects national resources Conserves and protects fish and wildlife Honors Native Americans and their habitats Manages 500 million acres or 1/5 of U.S. land including national parks Raises funds from minerals, grazing rights, energy, timber and recreational permits	Global warming and impact on resources and policy Determination of whether Keystone pipeline or other pipelines can be re-established Reassessment of development of Alaskan resources Drought conditions in California

	SIZE	BUDGET	DUTIES	KEY CHALLENGES
DEPT OF HOMELAND SECURITY	216,000 employees	$38.2 billion	Prevent terrorist attacks Consolidation of 22 former separate agencies after 9/11 including Secret Service, Coast Guard, TSA, FEMA and others. Responds to disasters Protects borders Enforces immigration	ISIS threats to homeland Protection of borders Illegal immigration
DEPT OF COMMERCE	38,000 employees	$6.5 billion	Promoting economic development Patents and trademarks Economic and demographic data Improving understanding of environment	Trade and currency issues with China Bringing cash of US companies and jobs back to the U.S.

Continued

	SIZE	BUDGET	DUTIES	KEY CHALLENGES
DEPT OF HEALTH AND HUMAN SERVICES	65,000 employees	$700 billion	Protects health of Americans Performs health and social science research Prevents disease outbreaks Administers health insurance Multiple divisions and agencies including National Institute of Health, FDA, Center for Disease Control	Administration of Obamacare and the dissolution of many of the state solutions Health care costs and viability of Obamacare
DEPT OF HOUSING AND URBAN DEVELOPMENT	9,000 employees	$40 billion	Responsible for national programs addressing America's housing needs Homes for low income families Fair housing laws	Housing Bubble

A review of the information provided above leads to some interesting insights. First, there is no relationship between the number of employees and the size of the budget of the department. Second, there is substantial overlap in the descriptions of the roles of the various departments, especially within the specific agencies. For example, multiple agencies have their hand in border security and immigration issues. Clearly a comprehensive immigration strategy must identify the specific roles and obligations of the multiple agencies involved. Numerous departments and agencies have a stake in energy development and the impact of developing pipelines. It's unclear why certain tasks are delegated to specific departments. For example, how many Americans would guess that the Department of Agriculture controls food stamps? It has no link to the Internal Revenue Service or the Social Security Administration. Should they work together? Could this lead to a reduction of some of the agencies?

It is impossible for voters to understand the layers of bureaucracy within the federal system. It is unlikely that even the President understands and could articulate the role of all of these bureaucracies. Perhaps some of this apparent mayhem is resulting in voters looking to outsiders to fix the federal government. Corporations continually reassess their own operations to increase their efficiencies. Shareholders don't allow corporations to duplicate operations or have departments that provide similar services. Voters shouldn't either. Perhaps it's time to "re-organize" and "right-size" this part of our Federal Government not specifically conferred by our Constitution.

CHAPTER 4

THE TRAITS VOTERS ARE SEEKING IN A CANDIDATE

As of November 2015, the candidates identified as "the outsiders" are leading the polls. While the percentages change on a daily basis, businessman Donald Trump, and surgeon Ben Carson, are among the preferred candidates of potential Republican voters. As we go to print, Marco Rubio is beginning to emerge as the establishment candidate. Voters must believe that these individuals possess specific qualifications that America needs in 2016.

The Research we conducted quantitatively with voters in November of 2015 indicates that voters believe the following traits are the most important for a Presidential candidate:

- Thirty-nine percent of voters are looking for Trust/Integrity/Honesty as the most important trait of a potential Presidential candidate. This may be due to a perception that the government has not been particularly open and transparent in recent years. It may also be due to the ongoing media discussion of Hillary Clinton's perceived issues with honesty and integrity. While this is the most frequently identified trait by all voters, 48 percent of voters over the age of 65 believe that Trust/Integrity/Honesty is important in 2016. Forty-three percent of women believe this is the most important trait of a Presidential candidate compared to 35 percent of men. Women and older voters are especially concerned about Trust/Integrity/Honesty.

- Nineteen percent of surveyed voters identified Leadership/Strong as the second most important trait of a Presidential candidate. This trait was the most important for the younger voters ages 18–45 (22 percent.) Twenty-three percent of men believe strong leadership is important compared to 14 percent of women.
- Other traits, while important, fell significantly behind Trust/Integrity/Honesty and Leadership/Strong. Eight percent of voters believe that the ability to negotiate or compromise is critical. Seven percent felt Values/Morals/Ethics are important. A similar percentage (7 percent) also believes that a candidate should be Smart/Intelligent/Knowledgeable. Tellingly, Political Experience was only the most important trait to 3 percent of voters. Two percent of voters believe that experience with World Affairs/Global Experience is important. Another 2 percent felt that Conservative/Religious/Believes in Constitution is fundamental.

Individuals participating in the quantitative study were asked a series of questions to understand why the "outsiders" appear to be doing so well among voters. These questions reviewed the importance of political experience as compared to overall intelligence as well as business and negotiation skills. While no one candidate may possess all of the characteristics desired by voters, perhaps a Republican Dream Team could provide a balance of these characteristics. Perhaps voters could trust that all of these important characteristics could be found around the table of a Dream Team Cabinet.

- **I believe a candidate should have some experience in politics before running for President.** Just over half of voters (53 percent) believe that a candidate needs to have political experience before running for President. Women felt more strongly that political experience is important at 61 percent compared to only 45 percent of men who felt political experience is important. Younger voters between the ages of 18–45 were more likely to believe political experience is important at 60 percent compared to only 49 percent of those over age 65.
- **Governors have the experience of running an organization as well as being familiar with politics and therefore are stronger candidates for President.** Seventy-five percent of voters agreed with this statement. This would indicate that governors might have a better chance at winning the nomination. As of November 2015, however, none of the Governors have been able to capitalize on this sentiment. Only Governor Jeb Bush remains in the top tier of candidates. While both men and women feel similarly regarding this issue, older candidates tend to be more supportive of this belief than younger voters.

- **Businesspeople are more experienced at cutting through the red tape and therefore will be more effective leaders.** Seventy-one percent of voters support this belief. Men and women feel similarly. Age is not a significant factor in whether a voter supported this belief.
- **Senators are more experienced at negotiating among various parties and therefore are more likely to be effective as President.** Marco Rubio, Rick Santorum, Rand Paul and Ted Cruz need to know that only 39 percent of voters believe that Senators are likely to be effective as President. Forty-five percent of women, however, are supportive of the capabilities of Senators compared to only 33 percent of men. The oldest voters, those over age 65, are the least supportive of Senators, with only 34 percent of voters agreeing with this statement compared to 42 percent of individuals between 45–64.
- **An individual who has demonstrated that he/she is smart will be effective as President.** This statement was meant to highlight whether or not voters believed that someone who has demonstrated that they are very intelligent, such as Ben Carson, could be seen as qualified based upon their intelligence alone. Forty-seven percent of voters supported this statement in contrast to the larger percentage that supported the concept of business skills. Men were more supportive of this concept at 51 percent compared to only 43 percent of women. Younger voters under the age of 45 supported this belief at 57 percent. Only 38 percent of voters over the age of 65 believe that brains are enough to be President.

- **The ability and willingness to negotiate is critical for the President.** Eighty-eight percent of voters support this belief. This may be because the existing President has not demonstrated an ability or willingness to negotiate with Congress or anyone else. This was the most highly supported belief tested within the quantitative research. There were only slight differences among segments regarding this attitude. For example, 90 percent of women supported this belief compared to 86 percent of men. Eighty-four percent of voters between ages 18–44 support this belief compared to 89 percent of voters over age 65.
- **Businesspeople are better negotiators.** While voters believe that a President needs to be able to negotiate, voters supported the concept that businesspeople are better negotiators than politicians, however, the support wasn't overwhelming. More than half of voters (56 percent) believe that businesspeople are better negotiators compared to politicians. Women support this belief more at 59 percent compared with 51 percent of men. There is little variation regarding this belief based upon age.

A recap of these beliefs highlights opportunities that candidates of various types can use to strengthen their own messages to future voters.

STATEMENT OF BELIEF	VOTERS THAT SUPPORT BELIEF
I believe a candidate should have some experience in politics before running for President.	53%
Governors have the experience of running an organization as well as being familiar with politics and therefore are strong candidates for President.	75%
Businesspeople are more experienced at cutting through the red tape and therefore will be more effective as leaders.	71%
Senators are more experienced at negotiating among the various parties and therefore are more likely to be effective as President.	39%
An individual who has demonstrated that he/she is smart will be effective as President.	47%
The ability and willingness to negotiate is critical for the President.	88%
Businesspeople are better negotiators.	56%

The results of the belief statements above are clear reflections of the political environment that has existed within the past eight years. Voters are very frustrated and Spectrem Group research consistently indicates that 78 percent of voters identify Government Gridlock as one of their greatest national concerns. Republican voters probably felt that government gridlock would end (or at least be lessened) when Republicans controlled both the House and the Senate. Alas, this has not happened. Even though many voters are blaming President Obama for the lack of compromise, Senators did not score highly in the beliefs articulated above. Governors are perceived as Washington outsiders who also have political experience. Based upon these findings, Governors should be leading in the polls. Instead, businesspeople or "outsiders" are at the top of the polls. Remember the importance of negotiation. Voters believe the ability to negotiate is critical and that businesspeople/professionals may be better negotiators. Perhaps this is one of the reasons that "outsiders" are leading in the polls in the Fall of 2015. Whether this is because of the sheer force of personality or something else, it will be interesting to see if Governors can reassert their potential before the primaries are over.

It is interesting to note that, according to *Wikipedia*, 17 U.S. Presidents served as Governor prior to becoming President. Sixteen Presidents were U.S. Senators. Eight Presidents were Cabinet Secretaries, with six serving as Secretary of State. Twenty-six Presidents were lawyers. Woodrow Wilson's occupation was an academic, Warren G. Harding was a business owner, and Herbert Hoover was a mining engineer. Harry Truman was a business owner, John F. Kennedy's only occupation was as a politician, and Lyndon Johnson was a teacher. Jimmy Carter was a farmer, Ronald Reagan an actor, and both George Herbert Walker Bush and his son, George W. Bush, were businessmen. Zachary Taylor, Ulysses Grant, and Dwight Eisenhower were in the military and went straight into the Presidency. They had no other political experience. The only President to go straight from the private sector to the

White House without any political experience was Herbert Hoover. It is interesting to reflect on this history as we approach the upcoming election with the realization that no one particular background for a candidate ensures a successful presidency.

CHAPTER 5

THE BUSINESSMAN/ WOMAN AND THE PROFESSIONAL

There are two business executives and one medical professional running for President. The media has recently adopted the term of "the outsiders" for these particular candidates. As of November 2015, two of these candidates, Dr. Ben Carson and Donald Trump, are riding high in the polls nationally as well as in many of the key states. Clearly, the "outsiders" have struck a chord with the electorate.

In The Research conducted by Spectrem Group, described earlier in this book, **52 percent** of respondents believe that businesspeople/professionals had the strongest skills for governing our country. In comparison, **37 percent** would vote for a candidate who was formerly a Governor while **11 percent** would vote for a candidate who was a Senator. It's important to note that the number of voters that support "the outsiders" does not vary by age group. Fifty percent of voters between the ages of 18 and 45 believe the non-politicians would be the best leaders and 55 percent of those over age 65 also support these candidates. Fifty percent of female voters and 53 percent of men indicate a preference for an outsider candidate.

Spectrum Group conducted focus groups with Republican and Independent voters as well. Focus group participants were asked their opinions of "the outsiders", and similar to the quantitative research and polling conducted by the national media, many individuals were enthusiastic about the outsiders. Participants responded as follows:

> *"I like the idea of outsiders because I like the idea of someone with fresh ideas who's not held to the old boys system that has been there forever. The one thing is foreign policy . . . although they could surround themselves with really good people. Foreign policy scares me."*

> *"A non-establishment person could go into office without owing anything to lobbyists or anyone."*

> *"Outsiders have generated interest in the election."*

We have long heard the cry government would be more effective if it were run like a business. The laser focus of a neurosurgeon as he tries to understand "the way government has always run" could lead to inquiries resulting in changes for the better. Consider a businessman who has successfully negotiated "the art of the deal"? Could this be a way to get Congress to work together? Or even a strong woman who has actually led a business and understands how to manage new initiatives and people. Maybe a business professional could re-examine the duplicate bureaucracies that exist? In fact the business and professional minds could bring an interesting perspective to all things about "the way we do business" in the President's Cabinet. These concepts resonated with focus group participants.

> "I would like to see someone with a business background go in there and run the country as a business as opposed to a political entity and hopefully have the acumen to surround themselves with good advisors to handle foreign affairs."

> "If one of the others or outsiders was chosen-how they would pick their team would be very different. It would be perhaps not politically one-sided. It might be what the country would need to bring the two parties together."

The following is a "resume" of the three outsiders currently running for the Presidential nomination: Donald Trump, Ben Carson, and Carly Fiorina.

Donald Trump is widely known for his books and for his popular television shows, *The Apprentice* and *The Celebrity Apprentice*. Ben Carson has indicated that he is the first to have separated the brains of conjoined twins. Carly Fiorina is the former CEO of Hewlett Packard.

BEN CARSON	Born 1951
Marital Status and Children	Lacena ("Candy) Rustin (1975–Present) 3 children
Religion	Seventh Day Adventist
Education	John Hopkins Hospital, Residency in Neurosurgery University of Michigan, M.D. (1977) Yale University, B.A., (1973)
Work Experience	Director of Pediatric Neurosurgery. John Hopkins Hospital, (1984–2013) First to separate conjoined twins, (1983) *Washington Times*, weekly opinion columnist (2013-2014) *Fox News* commentator
Additional Information	2001 Library of Congress Living Legend 2008 Presidential Medal of Freedom 2010 National Academy of Sciences Institute of Medicine 2014, Gallup Organization, No. 6 on list of World's Most Admired Men
Relevant Publications	*Gifted Hands: The Ben Carson Story* (1992) *America the Beautiful: Rediscovering What Made This Nation Great* (2013) *One Nation: What We Can All Do to Save America's Future* (2014) *One Vote: Make Your Voice Heard* (2014) *A More Perfect Union: What We the People Can Do to Reclaim Our Constitutional Liberties* (2015)

Sources: www.bencarson.com, www.wikipedia.com

CARLY FIORINA	Born 1954
Marital Status and Children	Todd Bartlem (1977–1984) Frank Fiorina (1985–Present) 2 stepchildren
Religion	Christian Non-denominational Raised Episcopalian
Education	MIT Sloan School of Management, M.S. (1989) University of Maryland, Robert H. Smith School of Business, M.B.A., Marketing (1980) Stanford University, B.A., Medieval History and Philosophy (1976)
Work History	AT&T Management Trainee (1980) SVP, Corporate Equipment and Technology (1990) Spinoff of Lucent Technologies from AT&T, led Corporate Operations Planned 1996 IPO of Lucent Technologies, most successful IPO to have occurred at that time Lucent Technologies, President of Consumer Products (1996–1999) Hewlett Packard, CEO (1999–2005) *Fox News*, Commentator (2007)
Political Experience	Republican National Committee Fundraising Chairman, 2008 Defense Business Board CIA External Advisory Board (2007–2009) Candidate for U.S. Senate, California (2010)
Other Experience	Chairman, Good360-donates merchandise to charities (2012) The One Woman Initiative-supports organizations in Muslim countries that provide empowerment to women
Relevant Publications	*Tough Choices: A Memoir* (2007) *Rising to the Challenge: My Leadership Journey* (2015)

Sources: www.carlyforpresident.com, www.wikipedia.com

DONALD TRUMP	Born 1946
Marital Status and Children	Melania Knauss (2005–Present)
	Marla Maples (1993–1996)
	Ivana Zeinickova (1987–1992)
	5 children
	7 grandchildren
Religion	Presbyterian
Education	University of Pennsylvania, Wharton School of Business, B.S., Economics (1968)
Work Experience	The Trump Organization, Chairman and President (1971–Present)
	TV Personality, *The Apprentice*
Political Experience	Contributor and Fundraiser for Republican Party (2014)
	Sarasota Republican Party, Statesman of the Year (2012, 2015)
Relevant Publications	*The Art of the Deal* (2004)
	Time to Get Tough: Make America Great Again (2015)
	Crippled America (2015)
	Trump for President: Why We Need a Leader, Not a Politician (2015)
	Numerous additional publications

Sources: www.donaldtrump.com, www.wikipedia.com

As noted, one of the greatest concerns about the skill sets of the "outsiders" is foreign policy.

> "*I can't see Donald Trump meeting with a bunch of Chinese and p***ing them off.*"

> "*My dad used to talk about Eisenhower being the best President ever. And I believe Reagan is the*

best President ever. And Reagan kind of went into office without foreign policy experience. Look who he surrounded himself with! I think if one of the non-establishment candidates could get in there and pay due diligence to their Cabinets and advisors. Then they could do a great job."

Clearly the ability for an outsider to demonstrate he or she could choose strong advisors, especially around foreign policy, will be a tipping point for that candidate.

"If we don't do something drastic here, we're going to be looking at a significantly different country."

CHAPTER 6

THE GOVERNORS

As you may recall from the previous chapters, Governors score highly with voters in terms of their ability to lead the country. In fact, **37 percent of voters believe that Governors are the most qualified for the job.** This compares to 52 percent who support the "outsiders" discussed in the chapter preceding this and only 11 percent who support Senators. Keep in mind, however, that three-quarters of voters indicated that they believed that Governors had the strongest skill set to lead the country because they have both executive leadership experience combined with political experience.

There are currently six Governors running for the 2016 Presidential nomination. Three candidates, former Texas Governor Rick Perry, Wisconsin Governor Scott Walker, and Louisiana Governor Bobby Jindal dropped out of the race.

The following is a recap of the qualifications of the Governors currently vying for the nomination.

JEB BUSH	Born 1953
Marital Status and Children	Columba Garnica Gallo (1974–Present)
	3 children
	4 grandchildren
Religious Affiliation	Roman Catholic
Education	University of Texas, Austin, Latin American Studies (1973)
Work Experience	Texas Commerce Bank, branch manager, Vice President (1974–1980)
	Codina Group (1980–1986)
Political Experience	Dade County Republican Party, Chairman (1985)
	Florida Secretary of Commerce (1986–1988)
	Campaign manager (1989)
	Candidate for Florida Governor (1994)
	George H.W. Bush campaign volunteer (1980 and 1988)
	Governor of Florida (1998–2006)
Other Experience	Established Points of Light Program (2000)
	Volunteered for Miami Children's Hospital and Dade County Homeless Trust and United Way (1994–1998)
Relevant Publications	*Profiles in Character* (1996)
	Reply All (2015)
	Immigration Wars: Forging an American Solution (2013)

Sources: www.jeb2016.com, www.wikipedia.com

CHRIS CHRISTIE	Born 1962
Marital Status and Children	Mary Pat Foster (1985–Present) 4 children
Religious Affiliation	Roman Catholic
Education	University of Delaware, B.A. Political Science (1984) Seton Hall University, School of Law, J.D. (1987)
Work Experience	Dughi, Hewit, & Palatuca, (Lawyer and Lobbyist (1987–2001); Partner (1993)
Political Experience	Morris County Board (1994–1998) Candidate for NJ Assembly (1995), unsuccessful Appointed U.S. Attorney (2001–2008) Governor of New Jersey (2009–Present)
Other Experience	
Relevant Publications	

Sources: www.chrischristie.com, www.wikipedia.com

JAMES STUART "JIM" GILMORE	Born 1949
Marital Status and Children	Roxanne Gatling (1977–Present) 2 children
Religious Affiliation	Methodist
Education	University of Virginia, B.A. (1971), J.D. (1977)
Work Experience	U.S. Army Intelligence (1971–1974)
Political Experience	Commonwealth Attorney (1987–1993) Attorney General of Virginia (1993–1997) Governor of Virginia (1998–2002) Chairman of RNC (2001–2002) Presidential candidate (2007) Senate campaign (2008)
Other Experience	Gilmore Commission, Chaired the Congressional Advisory Panel: Domestic Capabilities for Terrorism Involving Weapons of Mass Destruction (1999–2003) Chairman of RNC (2001–2002)
Relevant Publications	

Sources: *www.gilmoreforamerica.com, www.wikipedia.com*

MIKE HUCKABEE	Born 1955
Marital Status and Children	Janet McCain (1974–Present)) 3 children 5 grandchildren
Religious Affiliation	Baptist
Education	Ouachita Baptist University, B.A. Religion, magna cum laude Southwestern Baptist Theological Seminary, did not graduate
Work Experience	Televangelist, Staff (1976–1980) Immanuel Baptist Church, Pine Bluff, Arkansas, Pastor (1980–1986) Beech Street Baptist Church, Texarkana, Arkansas, Pastor (1986–1992) Arkansas Baptist Convention, President (1989–1991) The Huckabee Report radio show (2009–2015) *Fox News*, Huckabee Show (2008–2015)
Political Experience	Lieutenant Governor of Arkansas, (1993–1996) Governor of Arkansas (1996–2007) Presidential Candidate (2008)
Other Experience	
Relevant Publications	*Do the Right Thing: Inside the Movement That is Bringing Common Sense Back to America* (2008) *God, Guns, Grits and Gravy* (2015) *A Simple Government: Twelve Things We Really Need from Washington (and a Trillion We Don't)* (2011) *From Hope to Higher Ground: 12 Steps to Restoring America's Greatness* (2007) Numerous additional publications

Sources: www.mikehuckabee.com, www.wikipedia.com

JOHN KASICH	Born 1952
Marital Status and Children	Karen Waldbillig (1997–Present)
	Mary Lee Griffith (1975–1980)
Religious Affiliation	Catholic/Anglican
Education	Ohio State University, B.A., political science (1974)
Work Experience	Ohio Legislative Service Commission, Researcher (1974–1975)
	Fox News, Host of Heartland (2001–2007)
	Lehman Brothers, Managing Director, (2001–2008)
Political Experience	Administrative Assistant to Senator Buz Lukens (1975–1978)
	Ohio Senator (1978–1983)
	U.S. House of Representatives, Ohio (1983–2001)
	House Armed Services Committee
	House Budget Committee
	Created Balanced Budget Act of 1997
Other Experience	
Relevant Publications	*Courage is Contagious* (1998)
	Stand for Something: The Battle for America's Soul (2006)
	Every Other Monday (2011)
	Other publications

Sources: www.johnkasich.com, www.wikipedia.com

GEORGE PATAKI	Born 1945
Marital Status and Children	Libby Rowland (1973–present) 4 children
Religious Affiliation	Roman Catholic
Education	Yale University, B.A. (1967) Columbia Law School, J.D. (1970)
Work Experience	Plunkett & Jaffe, Partner Chadbourne & Parke, Partner (Post-Governorship)
Political Experience	Governor of NY (1995–2007) NY State Senator (1992) NY State Assembly (1984) Mayor of Peekskill, NY (1981)
Other Experience	Created the Governor George E. Pataki Leadership and Learning Center
Relevant Publications	*Pataki: An Autobiography* (1998)

Sources: *www.georgepataki.com, www.wikipedia.com*

Authors' commentary: It is interesting to note some differences between each of the governors vying for President. If you recall from earlier in this analysis, 17 Governors went on to become President.

- Three of the Governors are lawyers: Christie, Gilmore, and Pataki.
- The candidates with a career path without gaps are Christie and Pataki. Others have some gaps, however, the candidates may have been involved in other activities that are not especially easy to track. For example, Jeb Bush worked on multiple campaigns,

including his father's Presidential campaign. Additionally, Mike Huckabee has a career path with few gaps; however, it is a very different career path than some of the other candidates. This is not a positive or negative factor, simply a differentiator.
- Those candidates that can be perceived as having a somewhat privileged background include Jeb Bush and George Pataki.
- Candidates that are especially heavy in legislative experience include Kasich and Pataki.
- Christie has the greatest experience in working with governmental agencies.

Focus group participants were asked their opinions of the Governors and why the Governors might be successful as President. Responses were as follows:

"Experience. Actually having to do something. To run a state they have to cooperate with people and they don't get their own way 100% of the time. So if they are going to be effective they have to do something."

"They run a state but they're not actually any of the Washington insiders like a Senator or Congressman."

"Their terms of office are limited and when they are out of office they don't carry with them all of the benefits . . . like maybe a Senator . . . or White House china!"

"Accountable for their budgets that have to be balanced every year. Their results are measurable."

While not all Governors are held to the same standards—some states have term limits while others don't and some states require a balanced budget while others don't—overall, voters feel that Governors have a similar experience to what a President might encounter. The overall belief was that Governors are highly electable.

Thirty-five percent of surveyed voters between the ages of 18–44 felt that Governors have the strongest skills to run the country. The same percentage of voters over the age of 65 agreed. Forty percent of voters in the mid-range, those 45–64, support Governors as a leader.

As of November 2015, the Governors have not done as well in the polls. Yet because of the confidence voters profess regarding their capabilities, one of the Governors may be able to break through the clutter and still be able to win the Presidential nomination.

CHAPTER 7

THE SENATORS

Only 11 percent of voters believe that Senators have the requisite talents to become President of the United States. This is clearly a reflection of the generally negative opinion that voters have regarding Washington insiders and Congress, as expressed by the media, since the election of President Obama.

There are five current or former Senators running for President. In 2008, Senator John McCain ran for President against Senator Barack Obama. In 2004, Senator John Kerry ran against President George Bush. Throughout history, many Presidents, including some of the most highly regarded Presidents of both parties, previously served as Senators. John F. Kennedy was a Senator. Abraham Lincoln ran for the Senate, famously debating Stephen A. Douglas, but was ultimately defeated. (The debates made him famous enough to run for President.) In fact, as mentioned previously in this analysis, 16 Presidents served as Senators prior to becoming President. Only three, however, were Senators immediately prior to assuming the Presidency.

The following is an overview of the Senators currently running for the Presidential nomination in 2016.

RAFAEL EDWARD "TED" CRUZ	Born 1970
Marital Status and Children	Heidi Nelson (2001–present) 2 children
Religious Affiliation	Baptist
Education	Princeton University, B.A., Public Policy (1992) Harvard Law School, J.D., magna cum laude, (1995)
Work Experience	Cooper and Kirk, L.L.C., Attorney (1997–1998) University of Texas School of Law, Adjunct Professor (2004–2009) Morgan, Lewis & Bockius, L.L.P. Attorney (2008-2013)
Political Experience	U.S. Court of Appeals, Law Clerk (1995) U.S. Supreme Court, Chief Justice William Rehnquist, Law Clerk (1996) Office of Policy Planning, Federal Trade Commission, Director (1999–2003) George W. Bush, Domestic Policy Adviser (1999) U.S. Department of Justice, Associate Deputy Attorney General (2000) Texas Solicitor General (2003–2008) U.S. Senator (2013–Present)
Other Experience	Named "Conservative of the Year" by multiple conservative organizations
Relevant Publications	*A Time for Truth: Reigniting the Promise of America* (2015)

Sources: www.tedcruz.org, www.wikipedia.com

LINDSEY GRAHAM	Born 1955
Marital Status and Children	Single No children Adopted sister upon death of parents
Religious Affiliation	Baptist
Education	University of South Carolina, B.A. Psychology (1977) University of South Carolina, School of Law, J.D. (1981)
Work Experience	U.S. Air Force (1982–1988) Private Practice, Lawyer
Political Experience	South Carolina House of Representatives (1991–1994) U.S. House of Representatives (1994–2002) U.S. Senate (2002-Present) Committee on Armed Services Committee on the Judiciary Committee on Education and the Workforce Committee on International Relations Gang of 14
Other Experience	South Carolina National Guard, Guardsmen First Air Force Reserves, Colonel
Relevant Publications	*My Story* (2015)

Sources: www.lindseygraham.com, www.wikipedia.com

RAND PAUL	Born 1963
Marital Status and Children	Kelley Ashby (1990–Present) 3 children
Religious Affiliation	Episcopal
Education	Baylor University (1981–1984), no degree Duke University School of Medicine, M.D. (1988), Residency (1993) American Board of Ophthalmology, (1995)
Work Experience	McPeak Vision Center, Ophthalmologist (1993–1998) Graves Gilbert Clinic, Ophthalmologist (1998–2008) Private Practice, Ophthalmologist (2008–2011)
Political Experience	U.S. Senator (2011–Present) Committee on Energy and National Resources Education Committee on Health, Education, Labor and Pensions Committee on Homeland Security Committee on Foreign Relations Committee on Small Businesses
Other Experience	North Carolina Taxpayers Union (1991) Worked on multiple campaigns for his father, Ron Paul
Relevant Publications	*Government Bullies: How Everyday Americans are Being Harassed, Abused and Imprisoned by the Feds* (2012) *The Tea Party Goes to Washington* (2011)

Sources: www.randpaul.com, www.wikipedia.com

MARCO RUBIO	Born 1971
Marital Status and Children	Jeanette Dousdebbes (1998–Present) 4 children
Religious Affiliation	Roman Catholic/Southern Baptist
Education	University of Florida, B.A. Political Science (1993) University of Miami School of Law, J.D. (1996)
Work Experience	Broad and Cassel, Attorney (2004) Florida International University, Adjunct Professor (2008) Private Practice, Attorney (2008)
Political Experience	West Miami, City Commissioner (1998) Florida House of Representatives (2000); Speaker of House (2005) U.S. Senator (2011) Gang of Eight, Immigration Committee on Foreign Relations Select Committee on Intelligence Committee on Commerce, Science, and Transportation
Other Experience	
Relevant Publications	*American Dreams: Restoring Economic Opportunity for Everyone* (2015) *An American Son: A Memoir* (2013)

Sources: www.marcorubio.com, www.wikipedia.com

RICK SANTORUM	Born 1958
Marital Status and Children	Karen (1990–Present) 7 children
Religious Affiliation	Roman Catholic
Education	Pennsylvania State University, B.A. with honors, Political Science University of Pittsburgh, M.B.A. (1981) Dickinson School of Law, J.D. (1986)
Work Experience	Kirkpatrick & Lockhart, Attorney (1986–1990) Echolight Studios, Chairman and CEO (2014) Private Practice, Attorney
Political Experience	U.S. House of Representatives (1991–1995) U.S. Senate (1995–2007) Presidential Candidate (2012)
Other Experience	
Relevant Publications	*American Patriots: Answering the Call to Freedom* (2012) *It Takes a Family* (2005) *Blue Collar Conservatives: Recommitting to an America That Works* (2014) *Bella's Gift: How One Little Girl Transformed our Family and Inspired a Nation* (2015)

Sources: www.ricksantorum.com, www.wikipedia.com

Focus group participants weren't particularly supportive of Senators.

> *"How willing are they to compromise and work with the other side? I think they need some type of flexibility."*

"Too susceptible to lobbyists and other pressures. Not really for their constituents . . . .only when they need to be re-elected."

"Not like a governor who has to run a structure and get along with both sides."

"Just part of the Washington inside. Most of these people have no idea how people on the outside are making a living and trying to make a go of it."

"If we elect another Senator, I would expect that it will not be much different from what we have right now."

While the Senators are not leading the pack prior to the primaries of 2016, many of them are still popular with voters. Marco Rubio and Ted Cruz are popular with many voters and seem to be gathering strength in the polls. A Senator may still end up representing the Republicans in 2016.

Author's Comments: The Senators have more similar backgrounds to one another than either the Governors or the "Outsiders". Four of the Senators have law degrees and one has a medical degree. Most of the Senators also have significant political experience having worked their way up through the political system. Rand Paul, however, became Senator with relatively little political experience of his own. He was involved with his father's numerous campaigns. Marco Rubio has limited non-political experience. Rick Santorum and Lindsey Graham also seem to have short tenures actually practicing law. Ted Cruz has a strong resume outside of politics as well as within politics. These Senators need to do a better job of touting their resumes in a manner that will position them more effectively in the voters' minds rather than allowing them to be lumped in with the rest of the Washington malaise. Keep in mind that the ability to negotiate was perceived as important by voters. It is uncertain if Cruz and Paul, who position themselves as not part of the Washington inside, will be perceived as not willing to work with others or "negotiate".

CHAPTER 8

THE VOTERS IDENTIFY THEIR ISSUES

There is a delicate balance between a candidate's personality, his or her beliefs and the importance of the issues that influence voters. While it is easy to identify the most important issues that voters care about, even relatively unimportant issues can influence how voters respond to a candidate. Many of the participants in the focus groups (conducted as part of The Research discussed previously) indicated that everything about a candidate was "cumulative". Even if they agreed with a candidate on the major issues, it is still possible that if they disagree with a candidate on a number of non-critical factors, they still might choose not to vote for that candidate.

The rankings identified below are part of The Research conducted for this book and discussed in prior chapters. As you can see in the following charts, the top three issues identified were National Security and Terrorism, the Economy and the National Debt. It's interesting to note that in many of the national polls that have been conducted and are released on the networks, the Economy is generally identified as the most important issue. For this group of respondents, however, National Security and Terrorism was ranked just slightly higher. Please note that there is a 4 percent margin of error in the research. Therefore, the top three issues can be considered as equally critical. These results are also consistent with the focus group results in which the Economy, National Security and the Federal Debt were identified as the most important issues in the 2016 campaign. Please note that this research was conducted prior to the November 13, 2015 terrorist attacks on Paris.

It's important to understand that all of the issues ranked over 50 were considered important to voters. The only issues that scored less than 50 were Marriage Equality and Global Warming, often considered by much of the media to be issues more important to Democrats rather than Republicans.

Rank the Importance of Each Issue in the Upcoming Presidential Election

(0 = Not at all Important, 100 = Very Important)

National Security and Terrorism	90.06
Economy	89.06
National Debt	87.36
Jobs	83.41
Preventing growth of nuclear weapons in Iran	83.05
Immigration	81.93
Foreign Policy	81.11
Tax Reform	80.68
Obamacare Repeal/Reform	78.79
Government Gridlock	78.71
Viability and Reform of Social Security	77.42
Relationship with Israel	75.39
Hacking of Government Entities	74.76
Working effectively with European and other Allies	74.46
Effectively negotiating with/ controlling Russia	74.26
Effectively negotiating with/ controlling China	72.98
States Rights	71.80
Rising Food and Fuel Costs	70.17
Volatility of the Stock Market	65.38
Preservation of Traditional Marriage	61.43
Abortion Issues	56.82
Marriage Equality	42.95
Global Warming	42.36

Many of the issues overlap to some extent. For example, National Security and Terrorism (90.06), Preventing the growth of nuclear weapons in Iran (83.05), Foreign policy (81.11), Relationship with Israel (75.39), Working effectively with Europe and our Allies (74.46), Negotiating effectively with Russia (74.26) and Negotiating effectively with China (72.98) all ranked highly as key issues for the voters.

Focus group respondents had similar thoughts:

> "We used to be seen as strong or as a world leader. I don't know what we have to do, but something has to change."

> "I was watching CNN over in Europe when I was on a trip. They were making fun of us. That used to never happen."

> "My daughter was traveling this summer in Thailand. Because of her Wisconsin accent she was often mistaken as a Canadian. I told her to tell everyone she was from Canada because she would probably be safer as a Canadian than as an American."

Clearly the candidates running for the Presidency in 2016 must identify their strategy for strengthening the perception of the U.S. abroad. This is critical not only for national security but for the safety of Americans traveling abroad.

Other issues that overlap include the National Debt (87.36) and Tax Reform (80.68). In the quantitative survey these issues came in at No. 3 and No. 8. Focus group respondents also felt strongly about these issues, especially since the timing of the groups was at the same time that John Boehner had just been instrumental in passing an ongoing increase in the debt ceiling. Commentary included the following:

> "The 49 percent of people who pay taxes can't keep supporting the 51% who don't pay taxes. At some

point you reach a tipping point . . . .and it feels like we are almost there."

"Our children and grandchildren don't deserve this. If we don't do something soon, this won't be the same America we have always known."

The tax plans put forth by many of the Republican candidates are vastly different. They can be reviewed in Chapter 10.

The importance of the Economy (89.06) and Jobs (83.41) to voters must be underscored. Voters are seeking assurance from the candidates that they can strengthen the economy. While Spectrem Group research indicates that most U.S. households are feeling more positive about the economy than in the past, there is still a nervous feeling that causes those with investments in the markets to remain somewhat skittish. With the market volatility experienced in the fall of 2015, voters will be listening to see what messaging and solutions the candidates are offering. The respondents ranked stock market volatility at over 65 points. Some candidates have very strong messaging. For example, Donald Trump states regularly, "I will be the jobs President", while others have slightly less direct promises. Regardless of the specific language used, voters consider the Economy to be a critical issue.

While many of the candidates support repealing Obamacare, or at least revising it, the topic did not rank as highly with many of the voters as the issues identified above. Overall Repealing/Revising Obamacare scored 78.79. While still a high score, it did not supersede the Economy or National Security. For many voters, Obamacare is too far along and cannot be repealed, although most believe it can be revised.

> "I was meeting with my insurance agent for my business. The amount of increase that my employees are going to see is outrageous. I don't know how many of them will be able to handle it. The results are worse with Obamacare. On our existing plan the increase was really high, but if I put them on Obamacare, it would be a 30 percent increase!"

At a ranking of 77.42, Social Security was also an important issue to most of the respondents. As can be anticipated, Social Security reform was more important to the oldest respondents, however, the ratings were very similar among age groups. Those between the ages of 18–44 rated Viability and Reform of Social Security at 76.45, the 45–64 years old rated it at 77.18, and those over age 65 ranked it at 78.16.

The Immigration debate cannot be overlooked. Rated at 81.93, it was the fifth most important issue identified by voters. The importance of this issue does vary somewhat geographically, with voters in the Southwestern states rating it higher than in other states.

> "My son lives in Arizona. He says the crime rate has increased dramatically in just the past two years. At first he didn't pay attention to the immigration issue but now he feels it is in his face everyday."

Finally, State's Rights has emerged as one of the issues also identified by surveyed voters as fairly important

(71.80). It is important to note that many of the focus group participants felt passionately about this issue. At least 3 of the 10 were adamant regarding the importance of the separation of the state and the federal government while the remaining participants appeared supportive of their feelings.

> *"I want a candidate who clearly understands what this country was founded upon and how the states are responsible for some issues and the federal government is responsible for only a few. If a candidate doesn't seem to understand this . . . and there are some that don't seem to care . . . then I don't want that candidate."*

The respondents were asked to identify which issue they would rank No. 1 in relation to the 2016 Presidential race. The "Top Five" were as follows:

The Economy	18%
National Security and Terrorism	15%
National Debt	12%
Immigration	10%
Healthcare-Obamacare Repeal/Reform	10%

The importance of the Number One issues varied somewhat by age. Nineteen percent of those over age 65 felt that National Security and Terrorism was the primary issue for 2016 compared to only 9 percent of those between the ages of 18–44. Similarly, 15 percent of those between the ages of 45–64 identified the National Debt as most important compared to only 8 percent of the younger group and 10 percent of the older group. Note that The Research was conducted prior to the November 13th attacks on Paris. These acts of terrorism might influence the results.

Generally, voters indicate that key issues are more important to them than what could be defined as social issues. Most voters feel similarly to the focus group participant who said the following:

> *"How someone stands on the really big issues is what really matters. If they happen to be pro-choice and I am pro-life or something else like that then I will still vote for them if we agree on the Economy and National Security and other stuff like that."*

In contrast, other focus group participants agreed with the following:

> *"If I agree on the big things . . . that's good. But if I find that I disagree on a lot of the social issues, then it all adds up and I won't vote for the guy (girl). I mean . . . some of these things help define the character of the person."*

Finally, focus group participants discussed the importance of social issues in comparison to the primary issues identified above. While most individuals indicated that issues such as one's stand on abortion, or traditional marriage, or gay rights, or even Planned Parenthood, were not as important as the Economy, National Security, Taxes and related issues, the voters did indicate it is better if a candidate feels similarly to them regarding these issues. The one social issue that was a very "hot topic" for the focus group voters was Second Amendment rights. Even the Independents in the group were very supportive of the NRA and the rights of gun owners.

The importance of social issues was also tested with voters quantitatively. Forty-six percent of voters would not support a candidate who had a different view on traditional marriage. Forty-two percent would not support a candidate who had a different view on Abortion. Only 30 percent would vote against a candidate because they viewed Global Warming differently. Unfortunately, Second Amendment rights were not tested in the quantitative survey.

There were different viewpoints regarding these social issues based upon age. Almost half (47 percent) of voters between the ages of 18–45 would vote against a candidate with a different view on abortion. In contrast, only 37 percent of those over age 65 would allow abortion to guide their vote. Similarly, half of voters age 18–45, would vote against a candidate who had a different view on traditional marriage. Older voters did not feel as strongly regarding this issue. The survey did not ascertain the viewpoint of the voters regarding these issues, just whether the issues were important enough to sway their votes. It's interesting to note that there were smaller differences between age groups regarding Global Warming and Climate Change than with the other social issues.

Women were much more likely to feel strongly regarding a candidate's view on abortion when compared to men. Forty-seven percent of women indicated that a candidate's view on abortion would sway their vote compared to only

36 percent of men. Views between women and men did not vary significantly regarding Traditional Marriage or Global Warming and Climate Change.

While voters are open to varying opinions on social issues, these topics will influence their votes. Many voters in the research felt that the media highlights social issues to "stir the pot" and to make issues such as traditional marriage, abortion and climate change appear divisive. At the same time, voters claim to look past social issues, but these topics certainly color their ultimate opinions.

CHAPTER 9

THE VOTERS RANK THE CANDIDATES

The opinions that voters have of the candidates vary significantly based on the most recent media-based events. For those voters lucky enough to be in the early primary states, they have the privilege of actually being able to attend events where they are able to meet the candidates in person and to make their decisions based on actually hearing what the candidate may have said. The rest of the voting populace is subject to the whims of the media—hearing the sound bites that the media deems to be relevant rather than actual policy positions of the candidates.

Awareness and familiarity of the candidates has an incredible impact on how a candidate "polls" nationally. Lesser-known candidates find it much harder to obtain media coverage than someone like Donald Trump. In contrast, Ben Carson, who was unknown in 2014, has mounted an intense and successful social media and "field-based" campaign that has ultimately led to more media attention as he became one of the leading contenders.

The following chart, based on The Research conducted in early November 2015, highlights the familiarity and opinion of voters surveyed regarding the candidates.

CANDIDATE	FAMILIAR	RATING AS PRESIDENT
BEN CARSON	61%	74.11
MARCO RUBIO	50%	67.69
CARLY FIORINA	43%	63.58
JEB BUSH	63%	60.81
DONALD TRUMP	77%	55.92
TED CRUZ	43%	53.50
MICK HUCKABEE	47%	53.03
CHRIS CHRISTIE	53%	52.82
SCOTT WALKER	32%	51.13
JOHN KASICH	19%	50.89
BOBBY JINDAL	25%	45.63
RAND PAUL	41%	44.18
RICK SANTORUM	31%	42.99
RICK PERRY	38%	41.86
LINDSEY GRAHAM	24%	35.99
GEORGE PATAKI	14%	34.26
JIM GILMORE	4%	29.34

(0 = Not at all positive, 100 = Very positive)

In the research conducted in November 2015, voters were not asked for whom they believed they were going to vote. Instead, voters were asked about their familiarity of the candidates and how positively they felt about a candidate on a scale of 1–100, with 100 being the most positive. Candidates who dropped out of the race earlier were also included because it provided an interesting comparison to see how familiar voters were with these candidates and whether or not they were perceived more positively than some of the candidates that remain.

In addition to the quantitative research results, focus group participants were also asked about each of the candidates. This was some of the feedback received from average Americans who participated in The Research.

Ben Carson was perceived the most positively of all of the candidates in early November 2015. Sixty-one percent of voters in the quantitative Research were familiar with Dr. Carson. He was third of all of the candidates in terms of familiarity, following behind Donald Trump and Jeb Bush. He was ranked the most positively with a score of 74.11. While voters perceive Dr. Ben Carson positively, do they believe he can be President?

"Interesting."

"Not Presidential."

"Too polite."

"Intelligent."

"Needs to be more forceful."

Marco Rubio ranked second in terms of positive ratings at a score 67.69 in the quantitative Research. Fifty percent of voters indicated that they were familiar with the comparatively young politician. Personal opinions of focus group participants were primarily positive.

"Special interest guy."

"Too young."

"Like him."

"Articulate."

"On the ball."

"Interesting."

"In the future . . ."

"Dark horse."

"Compelling."

Carly Fiorina ranked third in positive voter ratings at a score of 63.58. Only 43 percent of voters, however, feel they are familiar with the former Hewlett-Packard CEO. Her positive ratings are likely to be related to her strong performance in the Republican debates. Little known during the first round of debates, Fiorina performed admirably and was able to grow her base enough to join the subsequent prime time debates and to increase in the polls. Voter feedback was as follows:

"Like her."

"Smart."

"Brilliant."

"Lacks political experience."

"Bright."

"Interesting."

"Incompetent."

Jeb Bush is one of the candidates with the highest familiarity ratings at 63 percent. Governor Bush is second in familiarity to Donald Trump but ranks more positively than Mr. Trump at a score of 60.81. Voters had a lukewarm response to Governor Bush.

"Maybe?"

"Established."

"Not inspiring."

"Working with the family name."

"Wishy-washy."

"Not strong."

"Boring."

"Re-run."

Donald Trump is the most highly recognized candidate of the vast Republican field with 77 percent of voters indicating that they are familiar with the real estate tycoon, author and reality TV personality. Despite his familiarity . . . or perhaps because of it . . . his ratings are less positive than the candidates identified above. At a rating of 55.92, he still rates more positively than many other candidates. Unlike Jeb Bush, voters had fairly strong opinions regarding Trump, both positive and negative.

"He just may win."

"Scary."

"Blowhard."

"Interesting."

"Tells it like it is."

"Too flamboyant."

"Very outspoken."

"Great hope. I think he has what we might need to get this country back on track."

Ted Cruz is familiar to 43 percent of voters. He is perceived positively at a score of 53.50. Those who feel they know Senator Cruz have very specific opinions:

"Not even on the radar."

"Too religious."

"No chance."

"He's sharp."

"Evangelical."

"Intelligent."

"Establishment."

Mike Huckabee is familiar to 47 percent of voters. Governor Huckabee, a winner in Iowa in 2008, hosted a popular show on Fox News for several years. He is positively rated at a score of 53.03. Voters felt as follows:

"Hot air."

"Too religious."

"Had his chance."

"Over with."

"Not qualified."

"*Been around too long.*"

"*Grandstander.*"

"*Old news.*"

Chris Christie, current Governor of New Jersey, is familiar to 53 percent of voters—a relatively high rating. He was ranked positively at a score of 52.82, very close to Huckabee and Cruz, and not far behind Trump. Voters expressed the following opinions:

"*His time in history has passed.*"

"*Not interesting.*"

"*Entertaining.*"

"*RINO (Republican in Name Only)*".

"*Too loud.*"

"*Acts before he thinks.*"

"*Not right.*"

"*Uninspiring.*"

"*Fat guy in a little coat.*"

Scott Walker, who is no longer a candidate, was known by 32 percent of the voters and ranked a 51.13 in the positive scale ratings, ahead of many candidates who remain in the race. Voters had interesting perceptions of Governor Walker:

"*Competent but not Presidential.*"

"*In the future . . .* "

"*Good Governor.*"

"*Excellent Governor but not national.*"

"*Would have done a good job.*"

"*Local.*"

John Kasich was only known by 19 percent of voters yet his positive rating was fairly high by those who did feel familiar enough to give him a rating. Kasich scored a 50.89. Governor Kasich received the following comments:

"*Never heard of him.*"

"*Need to know more.*"

"*Dumb.*"

"*I think he has gravitas.*"

"*I think his time has come and gone.*"

Bobby Jindal, Governor of Louisiana, was known by 25 percent of voters and scored a 45.63 on the positive rating scale. Jindal has withdrawn from the race. Voters did not feel they had enough information to rate him over a 50. Voter comments reflect this feeling.

"Too young, too inexperienced."

"Not well-established."

"Too established."

"Grow up."

"Not a chance."

Rand Paul was rated 12th in the positive rating score with a 44.18. Just over 40 percent of voters (41%) are familiar with Senator Paul.

"Down the road . . . ."

"Too flamboyant."

"Needs to be more tactful."

"Too out there."

"Libertarian."

"Interesting."

"Extreme."

"Not right for now."

"Too far to the right."

"Hopeful."

Rick Santorum is close to the bottom of the positive ranking score at a 42.99 and only 31 percent of voters were familiar with Senator Santorum. This is despite the fact that Santorum did very well in the 2012 primaries. Voters had few comments about Santorum.

"No chance."

"Too religious."

"Not new."

In fourteenth place was former Governor **Rick Perry** who has already withdrawn from the race. Perry had low recognition at 32 percent but a fairly high positivity rating at 51.13. Despite his withdrawal from the race, several voters had some positive comments.

"Old news."

"Too established."

"Underrated."

"Too nice."

"Quality."

"Honorable."

Lindsey Graham was not well known among voters at only 24 percent. His positive rating score may have been impacted by the lack of recognition at 35.99. Voters had the following comments:

"Yesterday's news."

"Isn't he a Democrat?"

"Surprised because when he talks I like what he says."

"Articulate."

George Pataki has low recognition among voters at 14 percent. His rating on the positive scale was only 34.26. Voters did not respond positively to Governor Pataki.

"Maybe next time."

"Not interesting."

"Yesterday's newspaper."

"Not right."

Jim Gilmore came in at the bottom of the recognition and positive rating scale. Only 4 percent of voters were familiar with Gilmore and he was not even given a score on the positive rating scale. Voters refused to fill it in due to lack of familiarity. Similarly, none of the focus group participants were familiar with Gilmore.

Several conclusions can be drawn from the material provided above. One of the more obvious findings is that many candidates that are not polling very high in the national polls as of November 2015 are still perceived as very viable candidates. Clearly Marco Rubio, Carly Fiorina, and Ted Cruz are highly regarded by a large number of voters. They are perceived as serious candidates. Most voters consider Jeb Bush positively even if he does not seem to inspire passion in voters.

Donald Trump, while recognized by most voters, is not the most positively ranked. At the same time, more individuals like him than those that don't, and commentary from voters indicates that he is seen as a leader and possibly a contender. In contrast, Ben Carson, who is both well-perceived and well-known by voters, receives commentary that he may not have a strong enough personality to become the President of the U.S.

Finally, there remain a number of candidates that are not well-known but who are not perceived negatively. John Kasich may fall in this group. Others are well known and still not popular. Surprisingly, this group may include both Mike Huckabee and Rick Santorum. Voters also have contradictory views. While Marco Rubio is perceived positively and described as young but articulate, Bobby Jindal was perceived as too young. The large number of candidates is confusing to voters but also may keep them interested in the election process as it proceeds.

So whom would voters choose? Keep in mind that The Research was conducted in November of 2015 and much will change before the primaries actually begin on February 1st of 2016. The Research has a margin of error of just over 4 percent.

Which of the following candidates are you most likely to vote for in the Republican primary/straw poll/election within your state (provided the candidates are still in the race)?	
Donald Trump	25%
Ben Carson	22%
Jeb Bush	15%
Marco Rubio	12%
Carly Fiorina	7%
John Kasich	5%
Chris Christie	4%
Ted Cruz	4%
Mike Huckabee	3%
Rand Paul	1%
Rick Santorum	1%

The remaining candidates—Jim Gilmore, Lindsey Graham, and George Pataki received no support in the quantitative poll.

While Donald Trump did not rank the highest on the positive feeling scale, he did receive the largest percentage of voters who would actually cast their ballot on his behalf. While Rubio and Fiorina are regarded more highly than Jeb Bush, they are more likely to vote for Bush. A balance of perceived leadership and strength of the candidate versus how much they really like the candidate as a person will determine the 2016 race. Voters are also conflicted by the need for political experience in a candidate versus the belief that an outsider may be more effective.

CHAPTER 10

THE CANDIDATES AND THE ISSUES

"One year out from the 2016 general election, voters in off-year races across the country on Tuesday offered some signs of things to come — and presented the presidential candidates with tea leaves to read as they sharpen their campaign strategies. By evening's end, Republicans were the ones crowing, as they scored a surprise win in a hotly contested governor's race in Kentucky while keeping control of the state Senate in Virginia, despite a big spending onslaught from former New York Mayor Michael Bloomberg's gun-control group." —(CNN 11/4/15)

As we go to press in late November 2015, it seems increasingly likely that a Republican could win the White House in 2016. In keeping with our Republican Dream Team concept we would like to make the process of vetting the candidates easier for our readers. Therefore we have provided information to facilitate your analysis of each candidate's position on various issues. In all cases we attempted to have the candidates validate the information included in this book. However, presidential campaigns are intense and at the time of publication no candidate responded to our requests to edit their information after numerous requests to all candidates. The National Republican Committee (NRC) reported they do not provide individual information on the candidates at the time of publication. They begin to compile this information after the primaries. Therefore, the information provided in this book should be regarded as a "sampling" of backgrounds and issues for each candidate. Any corrections identified after publication will be corrected on our website www.RepublicanDreamTeam2016.com. We encourage the reader to do more thorough research as needed on specific areas of interest.

A candidate might change his or her position during the writing of this book as they continue to add more detailed information on issues to their websites. For example, the terrorist attacks in November may force candidates to sharpen their positions regarding ISIS. In some instances the candidate's stance was condensed on a specific topic due to space. Therefore, we have included a link to each candidates' website at the bottom of their Summary Chart, located in Appendix C, to enable the reader to review every word the candidate has written on the issue.

The Spectrem Group conducted The Research previously identified to determine which issues are the most important to potential voters. This analysis was reviewed in Chapter 8. In this Chapter, the candidates' policies are reviewed and the number of voters that agree with a particular candidate's strategy is identified. Keep in mind that at this point of the election process, many candidates have not yet been able to get their messages out to the public. Therefore, most voters are not clear about each candidate's specific position on an issue. Those that have received more attention by the media and have been able to articulate their messages into sound bites have been the most successful at pushing their messages to the general public. For example, Donald Trump's position on immigration—"Build a wall"—is better known than the position of most of the other candidates. Additionally, some candidates have yet to articulate their opinions on various issues. When candidates have articulated unique ideas, those ideas have been highlighted where possible. Our hope is that candidates and voters alike will find this analysis helpful when making their ultimate selection of a candidate to support.

For the candidates who find the Dream Team concept intriguing, the next step could be for the candidates (and the Republican Party) to develop a comprehensive strategy based on the overarching themes presented on each issue. A set of actionable goals developed now and launched on January 21, 2017, when the Republican Party takes over the executive branch of government, would accelerate the time available to complete the work before the 2020 election cycle begins. It also gives hope for positive change to both conservative and moderate voters.

The following primary topic areas are addressed below:

- Economic Policy
- Taxes
- Immigration
- Foreign Policy/Terrorism
- Entitlements
- Social Issues

As mentioned above, each candidate's specific views are provided in more detail in the Appendix C.

A. ECONOMIC POLICY

All of the Republican candidates agree that the Economy is one of the most important issues of the 2016 election. Eighty-nine percent of voters are worried about the Economy, as indicated in Chapter 8, with 18 percent identifying this issue as their number one concern. As of October 29, 2015, the Bureau of Economic Analysis indicated that the GDP increased at an anemic rate of 1.5%. The candidates blame many factors for the stagnant economy and have suggested a variety of solutions among them excessive regulation, the complex federal tax code and government interference in areas best handled at the state level as overarching areas of concern. All candidates agree the national debt and federal budget are out of balance and unacceptable.

When voters were asked about which candidate's policies they felt would be the most likely to improve the economy, 36 percent of voters indicated that Donald Trump was the candidate with the best policies to improve the economy. Jeb Bush was in second place but at only 7 percent. Ben Carson's policies were supported by 6 percent of voters and Carly Fiorina was supported by 5 percent. In most cases, the voters could not articulate specific policies, but their belief is that their identified candidate would be the most likely to have strong economic policies.

The candidates have categorized their solutions for improving the economy and reducing the federal debt under the following broad categories:

1. Reduce the Size of the Federal Government
2. Eliminate the Federal Deficit
3. Create jobs
4. Trade
5. Energy policy

These policies, along with the minimum wage, will be reviewed in this section.

1. REDUCE THE SIZE OF THE FEDERAL GOVERNMENT

All of the Republican candidates agree the federal government has become too large. Candidates have made recommendations on reducing the number of federal agencies and employees paired with regulation reform to stimulate the economy. The following is a quick bullet point recap of some of the candidates' positions on reducing the size of the federal government. This is not a comprehensive reflection of the candidates' policies.

- **Jeb Bush:** Replace one federal retiree for every three who retire.
- **Ben Carson:** An across the board reduction of 10% of the federal workers.
- **Chris Christie:** "Regulatory Zero". Reduce an existing rule of equal cost for every new rule submitted.
- **Ted Cruz:** Abolish four unnecessary Cabinet agencies and the IRS. Institute Federal hiring freeze.
- **Carly Fiorina:** Cut regulations. Reform Fannie Mae and Freddie Mac. Repeal Dodd-Frank. Implement

zero-based budgeting. Every item is eliminated. Only what is needed is added back into the budget.
- **Lindsey Graham:** Restore Fiscal Discipline.
- **John Kasich:** One-year freeze on new regulations. Require mandatory cost-benefit analysis for new rules. Replace internally staffed administrative appeals process with independent reviews.
- **Rand Paul:** Audit Federal Reserve
- **Marco Rubio:** Permanently ban earmarks. Reform budget rules.
- **Rick Santorum:** Audit Federal Reserve

The Dream Team could agree upon some of these concepts and begin to "model" the suggested reforms before implementing them. This approach positions the team to immediately begin reducing and reforming the federal government after taking office.

2. ELIMINATE THE FEDERAL DEFICIT

As of the completion of this manuscript, the National Debt exceeds $18.6 trillion, according to the U.S. Debt Clock at www.usdebtclock.org. More than 87 percent of voters polled in The Research expressed concern about the National Debt with 12 percent of voters identifying it as their greatest national concern. When voters were asked which candidate's policies were the most likely to Reduce the National Debt, 29 percent indicated that Donald Trump's policies were the most likely to eliminate the federal deficit. Trump was followed by Ben Carson and Jeb Bush, both at 6 percent.

The following positions have been taken regarding reducing/eliminating the federal deficit:

- **Balanced Budget Amendment:** Supported by Jeb Bush, Ben Carson, Ted Cruz, Lindsey Graham, Rand Paul, Marco Rubio, Rick Santorum
- **Line Item Veto:** Supported by Jeb Bush

If a candidate is not listed above, it does not mean that he or she does not support these initiatives, it merely wasn't clearly reflected in the specific language available on their website.

3. JOB CREATION

Eighty-three percent of voters in The Research previously discussed in Chapter 8, indicated that Jobs are a critical issue. When asked which candidate they believed would have the strongest policies to Create Jobs, 38 percent of voters chose Donald Trump. Ben Carson was second at 7 percent while Jeb Bush was at 6 percent and Carly Fiorina polled 4 percent.

Below are some of the candidates' views on Job Creation including positions on Minimum Wage, and Foreign Labor.

- **Chris Christie:** Place a hard cap on the total cost employers pay to comply with all federal regulations. Make it easier for new companies to gain access to capital.
- **Ted Cruz:** Keep Internet free from regulation to spur entrepreneurial freedom.

- **Carly Fiorina:** Reduce regulations on small businesses to allow them to grow and increase jobs.
- **Rand Paul:** Spur private investment in poor neighborhoods.

The candidates have many views that support job creation, each approached from different viewpoints. Common beliefs support reducing taxes on corporations to allow them to invest in innovation and job creation.

Job Creation and the Minimum Wage

The minimum wage debate is a hot topic across the nation. In November 2015, the State of New York increased the minimum wage to $15 per hour for fast food workers to be phased in over three years in New York City and six years for the rest of the state. How do the candidates feel about increasing the minimum wage? Most of the candidates do not support increasing the minimum wage, however, many of them have not come out with clear rebuttals of an increase in the minimum wage (i.e. Ben Carson). Many of the candidates, including Fiorina, Christie, Carson and Trump, have indicated that creating better skills so that families don't need to rely upon a minimum wage is the most important goal.

- **Meritocracy program:** Carson, Fiorina
- **Increase minimum wage over time:** Santorum
- **Wage subsidies:** Rubio
- **States should control minimum wage:** Bush, Fiorina

4. TRADE

In earlier chapters, voters indicated that candidates with business experience were perceived as stronger negotiators. This would infer that businessmen/women would therefore be stronger at negotiating trade agreements.

President Obama is currently seeking to ratify the Trans Pacific Partnership Agreement ("TPP"). According to www.whitehouse.gov, the TPP protects worker's rights by banning child and forced labor, requiring a minimum wage, banning workplace discrimination, allows for unions to be formed, provides workplace safety standards and provides trade sanctions for violating labor rights. It also has significant environmental protections, protects customers from fraud and protects a free and open internet. TPP excludes China from the agreement. Opponents of TPP, including many Democrats, feel TPP will cost American jobs. According to Michael Schuman, in an article for www.Quartz.com (6/25/2015), there is a belief that TPP will lead to even greater outsourcing, although much of that outsourcing has already occurred. Additionally, Schuman points out that trade barriers are not great enough to offset the tremendous differences in wages between the U.S. and some of these other countries. The *Economist* (10/10/15) reports, however, that 18,000 individual tariffs will be reduced to zero, governments will be limited to the extent they may own certain businesses, and some agricultural barriers will begin to soften. The *Economist* indicates that the challenge with TPP is that many of the details are in the fine print of the agreement that has yet to be published.

What do the candidates think about the TPP?

- **Donald Trump** indicates it is "a terrible deal" in a Tweet on October 5, 2015
- **Carly Fiorina** indicated that TPP is "a mess" and "full of crony capitalism", according to *The Daily Caller* on 11/09/2015.
- **Jeb Bush** and **Marco Rubio**, according to CNBC (10/21/15), support the deal.
- **Lindsey Graham** has purportedly supported the deal in the past but remains silent at this time.
- **Ben Carson, John Kasich**, and **Chris Christie** also seem to support the bill but are awaiting the details.
- **Mike Huckabee** calls for "free trade" if it is "fair trade. Huckabee, along with **Ted Cruz** and **Rand Paul** feel that enough information has not been made available, according to the CNBC article cited above.
- **Rick Santorum** also seems skeptical.

And what about other trade issues? **Donald Trump** has a four-point plan for negotiating with China including: 1) bringing China to the bargaining table by "immediately declaring the country a currency manipulator; 2) protecting American ingenuity and investment by forcing China to uphold intellectual property laws; 3) reclaiming millions of American jobs and reviving American manufacturing by putting an end to China's illegal export subsidies; and 4) strengthening our negotiation position by lowering our corporate tax rate". Trump is the only candidate to specifically articulate a strategy for China.

5. ENERGY POLICY

> "The Obama administration's rejection of the Keystone XL pipeline Friday ends a seven-year saga with a declaration that the project is not in the national interest and would undermine U.S. global leadership in fighting climate change. The permit denial, which was cheered by environmentalists and lambasted by the energy industry, capped a politically charged review of the oil project that had escalated into a broader debate on climate change, energy and the economy." —(The Wall Street Journal, 11/6/15)

Full exploration of our energy resources adds to good paying jobs, energy independence and lower fuel prices. One area of consensus for all candidates was the approval of the Keystone XL Pipeline. Several candidates want to open up market access to all forms of domestic fuel production including off shore exploration of oil, nuclear and clean coal. Candidates want the ability to ship some of the increased fuel production by lifting the federal crude oil export ban. In keeping with the desire to divest responsibility from the federal government, Rick Santorum wants states to control sites for oil exploration, natural gas and hydrofracking.

The candidates were in disagreement on the repeal of the renewable fuel standard ethanol subsidy. According to the EPA website, the Renewable Fuel Standard program requires a certain volume of renewable fuel to replace or reduce the quantity of petroleum-based transportation fuel, heating oil or jet fuel. Companies that are able to blend fuels to meet certain standards receive tax credits.

Ted Cruz and Marco Rubio both expressly oppose the Renewable Fuel Standard ethanol subsidy.

B. TAXES

Every candidate has indicated that the federal tax system is too complex and must be simplified. Consistent with the other categories identified in The Research, the largest percentage of voters (25 percent) indicates that they agree with Donald Trump's tax policy. It is unclear, of course, whether the voters could clearly articulate Trump's strategy. Ben Carson was in second place at 10% and Jeb Bush's policies were popular with 7 percent of voters.

Tax policy is one of the areas in which the candidates have identified some of the most comprehensive plans. The policies are reviewed at a high level in this chapter. More information is available in Appendix C.

Most of the candidates agree that tax forms should be simplified to one system for all businesses and one abbreviated form for all individuals. Carly Fiorina suggests no more than a three-page form for individuals and Trump calls for a one-page form for 42 million taxpayers. Carson recommends that individual taxes should take no more than fifteen minutes to prepare. The reforms proposed by numerous candidates require closing loopholes in the current tax code for both individuals and businesses.

Individual Taxes
Proposed tax brackets:
Bush—3 brackets: 28%, 25%, 10%
Carson—10% flat tax, rebate for those at poverty level
Christie—Lower rates for every American

Cruz—10% Flat Tax
Fiorina—Lower rates
Gilmore—3 brackets: 10%, 15%, 25%
Huckabee—Abolish IRS, establish Fair Tax
Kasich—3 brackets: highest cut from 39% to 28%, all others cut
Paul—14.5% rate
Rubio—3 brackets: 15%, 25%, 35%
Santorum—20% flat tax
Trump—Four brackets: 0%, 10%, 20%, 25%

Alternative minimum tax retired: Bush, Rubio, Santorum, Trump

Corporate Taxes
In a 2015 Corporate Tax Rates guide published by Deloitte (www.2deloitte.com), the corporate tax rate of the U.S., which is 35 percent, places us in the illustrious companionship of Chad, Congo (Dem.Rep.), Guam, Equatorial Guinea, Guinea Conakry, Virgin Islands, Zambia and Zimbabwe. There are no countries higher than 35 percent. Comparative countries such as Japan have a 23.9% tax rate. Canada has a 15% tax rate. Russia and the United Kingdom share a 20% rate. China is at 25% and social democracy France has a 33.33% rate.

The Republican Presidential candidates are calling for a decrease in corporate tax rates. The following are the most popular proposals:
Reduce corporate tax rate to 14.5%: Paul
Reduce corporate tax rate to 15%: Gilmore (for business-created income), Bush (one-time repatriation of offshore assets at 10%)

Reduce corporate tax rate to 20%: Bush, Santorum
Reduce corporate tax rate to 25%: Christie, Kasich (repatriation of off-shore assets at lower rate), Rubio

Many of the candidates have additional proposals that are included in Appendix C.

C. IMMIGRATION

> "We must put an end to the unsustainable problem of 11 million illegal immigrants currently in our country living outside the bounds of legal structures. Status quo is de facto amnesty." —Lindsey Graham

Immigration has become a major issue in this election primarily because of strong opinions disseminated by some of the candidates as well as the challenges posed by national security threats, including terrorism. The Research indicated that 36 percent of voters supported Donald Trump's strong rhetoric regarding immigration that includes closing the borders and deporting individuals who are currently in the country illegally. Ten percent of voters indicated that Marco Rubio has the best policy towards immigration and 9 percent support Jeb Bush. The following is a synopsis of the issues and some of the candidates' opinions. More comprehensive positions are included in Appendix C.

SECURE THE BORDER

> "A 74% reduction in apprehensions was experienced when the National Guard deployed." —Rick Perry

The candidates generally agree that securing the border must happen before other immigration reform is initiated. While most agree that the border must be secured, the following proposals have been identified:

- **Jeb Bush** supports using new technologies to achieve continuous surveillance of the border, providing flexibility to the Border Patrol, and bolstering the infrastructure.
- **Chris Christie** supports building a wall where appropriate (urban areas), increasing manpower, and using advanced technologies such as electronic surveillance and drones.
- **Ted Cruz** authored legislation to triple the size of the Border Patrol.
- **Lindsey Graham** suggests an electronic entry-exit system to be mandatory at all international airports and seaports as well as enhanced training for the Border Patrol.
- **Mike Huckabee** believes the border should be secured by a fence and border control personnel must be increased.
- **Rand Paul** proposes building a fence within 5 years.
- **Rick Santorum** also proposes building a fence.
- **Donald Trump** wants Mexico to pay for a wall. Will triple the number of ICE Enforcement immigration law officers.

SANCTUARY CITIES AND CRIMINAL ILLEGAL IMMIGRANTS

In July, an illegal immigrant that had been deported five times (see cnn.com. Suspect-in-killing-of-san Francisco-woman-deported-five-times, 7/4/15) shot a young woman named Kate Steinle. Since that time, a bill known as "Kate's Law" has been proposed in Congress and voted upon numerous times. Bill O'Reilly, *Fox News* commentator, has been a big supporter of Kate's law. (See "I Haven't Given Up on Kate's Law, But I Have Given Up on Obama Admin, 11/18/25, *Fox News Insider*). Kate's Law proposes a mandatory minimum on an illegal alien who is deported but returns to the country. One of the reasons the initial proposal did not pass is because it prohibited federal funds for sanctuary cities. San Francisco is a sanctuary city. Sanctuary cities are those that don't enforce federal immigration laws. According to the *Washington Examiner* (July 8, 2015) there are more than 200 sanctuary cities in 32 states of the U.S. and Washington, D.C.

All of the candidates who have addressed this issue want sanctuary cities to be cut off from certain federal grant programs including law-enforcement and community development grants. (Christie, Rubio, Santorum, Trump). Rubio wants a public list to be created by DHS that identifies cities/towns as sanctuary jurisdictions. The list would also include the number of federal law enforcement requests that have been ignored by each city. The funds would be reallocated to local governments that allow law enforcement to work with federal immigration authorities. Gilmore believes that sanctuary cities should not be allowed.

Many candidates suggest that criminal background checks be done with a mandatory return of all criminal aliens. Ted Cruz urges the strictest enforcement of laws punishing those with prior felony convictions. Donald

Trump believes all criminals should be detained until sent back to their home country. If countries will not accept their criminals back, Trump suggests that visas for that country be canceled.

VISA OVERSTAYS

Regarding student visa overstay and asylum of refugee seekers, Rand Paul suggests creating a tracking system for holders of student visas as well as those who have been granted asylum or refugee status. Santorum and Christie propose that the U.S. should track overstays through the use of biometric systems and fining and removing anyone who overstays their visa. In contrast, Mike Huckabee would increase visas for skilled workers who enter the country legally, to increase U.S. competitiveness and to encourage legal immigration. Any illegal alien who enters the country must register with the U.S. government and return to his or her country within 120 days. If they fail to do so, they cannot return to the U.S. for 10 years.

LEGAL STATUS AND ASSIMILATION

> "Immigration without assimilation is invasion."
> —Bobby Jindal

Most candidates supported a pathway to legal status but not citizenship for immigrants already illegally in the country.

- **Bush** wants to require immigrants to pass a thorough criminal background check, pay fines, pay

taxes, learn English, obtain a work permit and to work with no benefit of government assistance and eventually earn legal status.
- **Cruz** wants to consolidate segmented visas, create real and transparent caps, eliminate the diversity requirements and treat all immigrants the same by not allowing per country caps.
- **Gilmore** believes that if a person ever came here illegally they should never be eligible for citizenship.
- **Graham** wants restitution from illegal immigrants who will be forced to pay steep fines, register with the government, pay taxes and get in line behind every single legal immigrant application for citizenship. Graham (along with Jeb Bush) insists that immigrants learn to speak English.
- **Trump** proposes that green cards be paused and employers forced to hire from the domestic pool of unemployed immigrant and native workers. He believes that American workers should be hired first and that petitions for workers should be sent to the unemployment office not the USCIS.

OTHER IMMIGRATION PROPOSALS

Trump proposes canceling J-1 visa programs for foreign youth and replacing it with a resume bank of inner city youth. He has also proposed the controversial policy of deporting all illegal aliens.

Trump, Bush, Christie, Graham and Santorum would implement a mandatory E-verify system to be used by employers.

D. FOREIGN POLICY, NATIONAL SECURITY, AND TERRORISM

> "We must address Islamic terrorism and protect our country first. I will lead by example, as I always have, by vowing to defeat ISIS, stop illegal immigration and the Syrian refugee program, secure our border and bring real change to Washington."
> —Donald Trump radio ad 11/20/15

The primary role of the U.S. President, as defined in our Constitution, is national security (See Chapter 3). As of the publication of this book, the Senators in particular have written extensively on foreign policy issues on their websites. We encourage voters to review the candidates' websites. All candidates, however, support a coherent, comprehensive, unified global strategy that secures our interests and, for some, our values around the world. There was significant agreement on foreign policy being built on President Reagan's principle of "Peace through Strength."

In Chapter 8, The Research conducted for this book highlighted the issues over which voters had the greatest concern. The largest percentage of voters identified National Security and Terrorism as a concern, however, the Economy just slightly edged out National Security as the #1 concern. The Research, however, was completed prior to the November 13th terrorist acts in Paris. It is anticipated that National Security would clearly overcome the Economy at this juncture. Even prior to the attacks, 19 percent of voters felt that Donald Trump would have the strongest policies to protect them against terrorism. Eleven percent chose Jeb Bush and 6 percent chose each

Ben Carson and Chris Christie. Feelings were similar regarding which candidates would have the strongest strategies to address ISIS with 17 percent choosing Donald Trump and 10 percent choosing Jeb Bush. Six percent chose Marco Rubio.

ISIS

ISIS has become one of the leading issues of the election since the Paris attacks, and subsequent terrorist activities. Because the candidates have multiple ideas and stances regarding this issue, the following table reviews some of their ideas and policies.

CANDIDATE	ISIS POLICY/STRATEGY
BUSH	Give Kurds decisive military power against ISIS
	Support moderate groups to come together as one force while improving recruitment and retraining to form forces to go against ISIS in Syria
	Establish safe zones to protect Syrians from ISIS and Assad
	Create a no-fly zone
CARSON	Destroy their Caliphate-especially in Iraq-Take the energy field that is outside of Anbar province
	Destroy them before they destroy us-Provide financial support to countries like Jordan to assist with the refugees but do not allow them to come to the U.S.
CHRISTIE	Empower the intelligence community
CRUZ	Revoke citizenship of anyone fighting or supporting ISIS
FIORINA	Support and assist allies in the Middle East by providing equipment, resources and intelligence

CANDIDATE	ISIS POLICY/STRATEGY
GILMORE	Support moderate Muslim leaders. Strengthen intelligence capabilities
GRAHAM	Use military options, if necessary
HUCKABEE	Keep all options on the table to defeat Radical Islam
KASICH	Work with the French on logistics
	Build a coalition similar to NATO but including Middle Eastern countries.
	No fly zones in Syria, Turkish border and Jordanian border
PATAKI	Must attack ISIS in Iraq and Syria
	Do not allow them to train and recruit to plan more Paris-like attacks
	Stop taking refugees until vetting process is fixed
PAUL	Only use military as a last resort and with approval of Congress
RUBIO	Expand airstrikes in Syria and Iraq.
	Deploy U.S. Special Ops
	Train Syrian rebels and develop safe zones in Syria
	Provide arms to Sunni tribal and Kurdish forces
	Prevent jihadists from traveling from homes, battlefields and to U.S.
	Strengthen intelligence, especially around "lone wolf" attacks and throughout U.S.
SANTORUM	Launch a major offensive against ISIS-Obama is running a PR campaign
TRUMP	Bomb ISIS

Rubio states that we need to "Name the enemy: Radical Islam". Fiorina differentiates ISIS from Islam with the description "Culture in Islam was welcoming and various religions were respected and science/arts celebrated." She also believes the United States should be committed to the destruction of ISIS and that Radical Islam commits murder/mayhem and reminds us that any religion can be abused.

The candidates have addressed the defeat of ISIS generally and then have given specific recommendations for the countries of Syria and Iraq where ISIS is currently operating. They are in consensus that all means should be used to keep ISIS terrorists from being able to enter the United States and prevent ISIS from inspiring "Lone Wolf" attacks. Rubio states specifically that ISIS should be prevented from entrenching in Afghanistan, Libya and Jordan. He further states the United States should coordinate with regional allies to target ISIS' financial reserves with sanctions, freeze assets and undermine ISIS' ability to exploit oil resources. Donald Trump has also indicated that the U.S. should focus on bombing ISIS' oil supplies.

UNITED STATES MILITARY

In recent years, the U.S. has spent fewer dollars on building the capabilities of the U.S. Military. There is strong consensus among the Republican candidates that appropriately funding and modernizing our military would increase our military size and readiness. Chris Christie specifically calls for the Repeal of the 2011 budget control act and the restoration of funding levels to what Secretary Gates proposed in 2012. Christie believes that additional capital is needed to innovate to fight the battles of the future with new generations of weapon systems to protect our interests on every front (ground, sea, air and new frontiers further out). Lindsey Graham also wants to end across-the-board military cuts and assert a global leadership role. Mike Huckabee believes in rebuilding America's military superiority and avoiding conflict by having a lethal fighting force. John Kasich's approach focuses on rebuilding the Navy.

SUPPORT OF ISRAEL AND THE IRAN NUCLEAR DEAL

In July, the U.S. signed a deal with Iran that will allow Iran to have the ability to create a nuclear weapon in 10 years. This deal was polarizing among the parties and also threatened America's relationship with Israel. In March, Israel's Prime Minister Benjamin Netanyahu addressed the U.S. Congress and asked them to oppose the deal, which the Congress did. However, they could not achieve a veto-proof majority. Israel, a democratic nation, is our key ally in the Middle East. Israel is described by Ben Carson as our "bulwark of the Middle East" and states, "We could never let Israel's enemies believe that the United States' deep commitment to Israel's peace and security will waiver". All of the candidates support maintaining our strong relationship with Israel and Israeli President, Benjamin Netanyahu. Fiorina said her first call after winning the election would be to Netanyahu to tell him "We stand with the State of Israel". Strong, affectionate words like "proud supporter," and "longtime friend" were used to describe the U.S. relationship with Israel. The candidates have expressed concern that this special relationship with Israel and President Netanyahu has been eroded during President Obama's administration. Graham states, "Any international institution of which the United States is a member and a funding source, should refrain from becoming a tool for undermining Israel". Marco Rubio indicates that he will defend Israel's efforts to combat terrorism and fight efforts to de-legitimize the Jewish State.

None of the Republican candidates support the Iran Nuclear Deal. Policies and positions are as follows:

- **Marco Rubio** has a three-point plan beginning with forcing Iran's leaders to make a choice between having a nuclear weapons program or having an economy. He would back this up with a credible threat of "military force if Iran decides to ramp up its program." He will work with Congress to impose tougher sanctions on Iran for its support of terrorism and human rights abuses, rather than treating Congress as an "afterthought".
- Now that the deal is in force, **Carly Fiorina** wants to ensure adequate Inspection regiments exist, that the goals of the agreement are remembered and that the United States "sticks with them; be prepared to walk away; and strike a new deal unless every nuclear power plant and military base with anytime anywhere inspections is available." Anticipating that Iran may not comply with the deal, she wants to make sure "it is as hard as possible for them to move money around the global financial system".
- **Mike Huckabee** reinforces that Iran can't be trusted and cannot be given the capacity to end up with a nuclear weapon.
- **Donald Trump**, on the other hand, does not believe we should reveal our plans to address issues with Iran by talking about it. However, he describes the current deal as "horrific."

EUROPEAN AND OTHER ALLIES

As the threat of terrorism rears its ugly head in Europe, the Republican candidates overwhelmingly reiterate that the U.S. must stand with its European Allies.

Ben Carson: "We must lead our allies, both NATO and non-NATO alike from a position of strength."

Lindsey Graham: "Many of our closest allies have been alienated or disregarded during the Obama years. Our friends and would-be partners have seen that our enemies get better treatment and more serious regard than those who have stood with us. They question our loyalty and our commitment to lead, and as a result, have good reason to doubt the benefits of working together in common purpose. It is time to re-engage with our allies and demonstrate renewed commitment to global security, stability, and prosperity."

Chris Christie: "We need to stand with our allies and stand up to our adversaries". He wants to "encourage NATO Allies to invest more in their own defense."

SYRIA AND IRAQ

Although candidates provide some comments on these countries, two candidates, Bush and Rubio, present detailed plans relating to these countries. Instead of reproducing their plans in this chapter we refer you to their Issue Summaries in the Appendix.

RUSSIA

Five candidates focus specifically on Russia in their foreign policy comments.

- **Ben Carson** describes President Vladimir Putin and Russia as "dangerously belligerent and destabilizing Ukraine, endangering Europe in the process and continuing to fuel destabilization of the Middle East . . . All options should remain on the table when dealing with international bullies such as President Putin."
- **Carly Fiorina** believes Russia's actions have been "predictable" and that we need a President who will "push back". She would not "talk with him", instead she would begin "rebuilding the sixth fleet; rebuild the missile defense program in Poland; conduct more military exercises in the Baltic State and ramp up troop presence in Germany."
- **Marco Rubio** has a five-point plan including: defend and restore Ukrainian sovereignty; protect Europe from further Russian aggression; reclaim leadership in Syria; highlight Russian arms control violations; and advocate for Russian journalist, dissidents, and democracy activists.
- **Chris Christie** believes that the United States should "stand with the Western Alliance against Russian aggression".
- **Mike Huckabee** states we should show "resolve to prevent Russia from repeating their annexation formula used in Georgia and Ukraine."

CHINA

Four candidates specifically address China in their foreign policy agenda.

CANDIDATE	POSITION
Donald Trump	Declare China as a currency manipulator
	Force China to recognize intellectual property laws and stop their practice of requiring U.S. companies to share proprietary technology
	End Chinese illegal export subsidies and lax labor and environmental standards
	Lower our corporate tax rate and National Debt so China cannot blackmail the U.S.
	Bolster U.S. military presence in the South China Sea
Marco Rubio	Restore U.S. strength so it remains a Pacific power
	Protect the U.S. economy.
	Protect freedom and human rights both inside China and on its periphery
Mike Huckabee	Rebuild military to contain China
	Emphasize offensive cyber-warfare Capabilities to effectively hack China
	Stand unapologetically for Chinese democracy
Carly Fiorina	Decisively show China that building military bases in South China Sea is unacceptable

CYBER-ATTACKS

On November 22, 2014, Sony Pictures was hacked due to its upcoming release of a movie entitled *The Interview*. The movie painted an unflattering picture of North Korea's leader. It was believed the North Korea was behind the attack. During the course of 2015, multiple corporations and governmental entities were hacked. On July 9, 2015, the *New York Times* indicated that the records of 21.5

million people had been exposed due to the hacking of governmental computers. China was blamed for the hacking yet nothing has really been done to address the issue. Clearly hacking is a new form of warfare that the U.S. must learn to fight to protect not only individual records but the financial system and our military intelligence system.

How have the candidates addressed this threat?

Jeb Bush: Work with the private sector. Hold government agencies accountable for hacking. Restore funding to FBI, Intelligence Community and Defense Department to develop weapons and strategies to address the threat. Develop cyber security agreements with allies around the world.

Chris Christie: Cyber warfare is reality. Need to defend against threats and develop offensive capabilities. Strike back when necessary to develop digital balance of power.

Mike Huckabee: Hack the Chinese government and hack the cell phones of prominent Communist party leaders.

E. ENTITLEMENTS

Many candidates chose not to address entitlements on their websites. As we stated at the start of this chapter we are primarily sourcing the candidates' campaign websites for information on the issues due to the continually changing information and news coverage. To the extent additional information is available, we have attempted to source that information.

SOCIAL SECURITY

Good news! According to the Center on Budget and Policy

Procedures, in a report released in July 2015, Social Security will not go bankrupt in 2033. Instead, it will go bankrupt in 2034. Hooray! Voters in The Research conducted for this book indicated that Donald Trump is the candidate most likely to solve the Social Security crisis, but only at 14 percent, lower than some of the other categories polled. Eleven percent of voters believe Ben Carson is the candidate with the knowledge to resolve the Social Security issue and 10 percent support Jeb Bush.

How do the Republican Presidential candidates plan to solve the Social Security crisis? The most common solutions include increasing the retirement age and implementing means testing. These proposals would be implemented gradually and would not impact existing seniors or most of the Baby Boomers.

- **Lindsey Graham** describes entitlement programs as the greatest "threat to our long-term fiscal health and the national debt" yet recognizes they are vital programs to "seniors and the most vulnerable in society." Graham calls for meaningful reforms to ensure they remain "viable for current and future generations".
- **Marco Rubio** proposes gradually increasing the retirement age for future retirees to keep up with changes in life expectancy. Rubio also agrees with reducing the growth in benefits for upper-income seniors while strengthening the program for low-income seniors.
- **Chris Christie** suggests a "phased-in plan" for future retirees with income outside of Social Security of up to $80,000 a year receiving full benefits; those

above $80,000 a year receiving benefits on a sliding scale and benefits phase out entirely for those that have $200,000 a year of outside income. For couples, these thresholds would be higher. Christie also wants to increase the retirement age to 69, gradually implementing the change beginning in 2022.

- **Rick Santorum** supports reform and strengthening the program so it is fiscally sustainable for seniors and future generations. He does not, however, offer any specific details.
- **Carly Fiorina** indicates she "will not talk about Social Security and Medicare until the government can execute with excellence, perform its responsibilities with excellence; serve the people who pay for it with excellence."
- **Mike Huckabee** proposes to prosecute Medicare fraud, grow the economy to feed the Social Security Trust Fund and ensure everyone is actually paying into the system.
- **Rand Paul** supports gradually increasing the retirement age and implementing means testing in the future.

OBAMACARE

As of November 20, 2015, *USA Today* reported that United Healthcare indicates it can no longer support Obamacare exchanges due to the low enrollment and high usage. Other large insurers are also rumored to be considering the same strategy. Obamacare has been a hot topic for Republicans and the Presidential candidates have strong opinions regarding this legislation.

Ted Cruz authored the Obamacare Repeal Act and views Obamacare as the "largest regulatory challenge facing our nation, which has resulted in killing jobs, cutting workers' hours, and causing millions of Americans to lose their doctors or healthcare." Fifty percent of the candidates addressed Obamacare on their websites and have called for a full repeal of the $1.2 trillion program. These candidates would make the states responsible for healthcare. Rand Paul and Lindsey Graham advocate that Obamacare is the result of a health care system that was over-regulated and in need of serious market reforms. Most candidates included features such as Health Savings Accounts (HSAs) and focused on maintaining wellness as part of their plan.

Rubio recommends Medicare reform and calls for "shuttering Obamacare's Independent Payment Advisory Board", "strengthening Medicare Advantage" and making the "Medicare trust fund permanently solvent." He wants to give seniors more options to "choose the coverage they need and the doctors they see."

Kasich calls for "Patient Centered Primary Care" and sharing of savings with providers whose work helps improve health and hold down costs. He also wants to move to an "Episode Based Payment" system where providers work as a team to control costs and maximize quality.

REPEAL OBAMACARE	REVISE OBAMACARE	OTHER PROPOSALS
Bush, Cruz, Graham, Huckabee, Kasich, Paul, Santorum	Gilmore, Rubio	Carson, Fiorina

F. SOCIAL ISSUES

As discussed in previous chapters, most voters won't vote for a candidate based only on that candidate's stance on social issues, however, those issues do matter when comparing candidates against one other. Some voters have especially strong feelings regarding some of the following social issues.

GUN CONTROL

> "When you look at Paris, you know, the toughest gun laws in the world, nobody had guns except for the bad guys, nobody," Trump said at a campaign rally in Beaumont, Texas, on Saturday, (November 14, 2015). "Nobody had guns, and they were just shooting them one by one."
> —Donald Trump, The Hill, 11/14/15

All of the candidates who addressed this issue on their website are strong proponents of the Second Amendment and a law-abiding citizen's right to bear arms to protect themselves from both foreign and domestic threats. (Rand Paul, Marco Rubio, Donald Trump, Rick Santorum, Carly Fiorina, Lindsey Graham, Mike Huckabee, John Kasich, Jim Gilmore, Ben Carson, Ted Cruz). Candidates believe in a reasonable expansion of rights that would allow permit holders to carry their firearms. Candidates want every state and the District of Columbia to honor the concealed permits issued by every other state. Candidates agree that the government has no business dictating what types of firearms law-abiding citizens should be allowed to own. They oppose new gun restrictions, registrations, regulations and mandates. The candidates called for prosecution in federal court of violent felons using guns to commit crimes, fixing our broken Mental Health System, and repairing the broken system of background checks.

SUPPORT OF TRADITIONAL MARRIAGE

Another "hot topic" is the recent decision of the United States Supreme Court to recognize same-sex marriage. Despite the fact that this has become the law of the land, many of the candidates still believe strongly in traditional marriage.

Ted Cruz States should have the right to define marriage

Carly Fiorina Supports civil unions for purposes of benefits. Believes marriage is a spiritual foundation for only a man and a woman.

Lindsey Graham Believes states should define marriage and defends traditional marriage but realizes can't overturn Supreme Court decision.

Rick Santorum Has fought against same-sex marriage

ABORTION/RIGHT TO LIFE

"50 million children have been killed since Roe vs. Wade." —Rand Paul

Each of the nine candidates who address abortion on their website are "pro-life" and against partial birth abortions. Huckabee imposed a ban on partial birth abortions while Arkansas Governor. He also established waiting periods, parental notification and supports the ability for women to take newborn babies to a hospital or fire station without being prosecuted for child abandonment. Santorum authored legislation outlawing partial birth abortion. Kasich voted to outlaw partial birth abortion and Cruz defended the federal law in front of the Supreme Court. Cruz believes abortion is a state issue. Graham wants the Graham 20-Week Pain Capable Unborn Child Protection Act to be endorsed. Huckabee, Kasich and Paul oppose public funding for abortion and Cruz successfully defended prohibiting State funds for abortions.

Many believe abortion should be a state issue and Paul would like to restrict the Federal Courts from hearing cases like Roe v. Wade. Most candidates support withholding federal funding to facilities that provide abortions.

GLOBAL WARMING

"Follow the Scout rule: 'Leave the earth better than we found it.'" —Mike Huckabee

"Washington said they were going to manage your

water—population has doubled in 40 years and no new reservoirs have been built" —Carly Fiorina

Only three candidates address global warming on their websites. Huckabee states it is a "moral issue." Gilmore believes climate change is a reality and cannot be solved by America alone. He states, "no treaties, laws or regulations that strangle our economy with the goal of reducing global carbon emissions" should be allowed. Fiorina indicates global warming is an "example of politicians' ideology trumping others livelihoods."

CHAPTER 11

VOTERS AND THE DREAM TEAM CONCEPT

The number of interesting and talented candidates in the 2016 election allows voters to be more selective than usual as they begin to contemplate how to cast their vote in the upcoming primaries. Many of the voters will thoughtfully review the candidates and their positions while others will listen to the sound bites reported in the media and make their decision based on that limited information. Sometimes a voter may feel as if the candidate they like the best may not ultimately be popular enough to win the nomination and may feel as if they must vote for a more viable candidate . . . or maybe they won't vote at all.

The Republican Dream Team concept encourages the candidates to band together to present a "team" to the voters . . . perhaps identifying a Vice President, Secretary of State, Secretary of Health and Human Services as well as other Cabinet appointees prior to the election . . . or even the primaries. A Dream Team concept could increase overall voter support because even if a voter's favorite candidate doesn't win the nomination, the talents and the proposed reforms touted by that candidate can still be used to overcome the obstacles faced by our country. It also helps government to look more like a business, placing individuals with specific goals and talents in charge of administrative industries that are bloated and inefficient.

How did voters respond to the Dream Team concept? Voters were asked "*If a candidate was to identify his or her potential Cabinet nominees should they receive the nomination, would that make a candidate more appealing?*" Sixty-seven percent of voters indicated that they find the idea appealing. Younger voters ages 18–44 were the most likely to support the concept at 71 percent. Those between the ages of 45-65 supported the concept at 68 percent while those over age 65 were at 64 percent.

Focus group respondents had additional input:

"*I like it. It's more like a business works.*"

"*I would like it because you could see the quality of the people that they would bring to the table.*"

"*What is the political advantage?*"

"*It would be useful information for voters to have.*"

"*I don't think Trump would ever do this. I think his Kindergarten report card probably said 'Does not play well with others'*".

"*It would be nice to know who they might surround themselves with . . . but they might choose people just to get votes.*"

The Research presented the names of the candidates

(including candidates that have withdrawn from the race) and the potential Cabinet positions to see if voters could mix or match some of the candidates to some of the Cabinet positions that they might effectively manage. In many cases there were relatively low ratings, therefore, only the candidates that scored the highest percentages are mentioned.

CABINET POSITION	CANDIDATES CONSIDERED
Secretary of State	Jeb Bush 11% Carly Fiorina 10% Ben Carson 7%
Attorney General (Dept. of Justice)	Chris Christie 12% Ted Cruz 8% Jeb Bush 6%
Secretary of Transportation	Chris Christie 9% Jeb Bush 3%
Secretary of the Treasury	Donald Trump 19% Carly Fiorina 12% Ben Carson 4% John Kasich 4%
Secretary of Agriculture	Mike Huckabee 5% Rick Perry 5% Jeb Bush 4%
Secretary of Commerce	Donald Trump 16% Carly Fiorina 8%
Secretary of Defense	Jeb Bush 8% Lindsey Graham 8%
Secretary of Homeland Security	Chris Christie 7% Donald Trump 6% Jeb Bush 6%

Continued

CABINET POSITION	CANDIDATES CONSIDERED
Secretary of Health and Human Services	Ben Carson 19%
	Jeb Bush 11%
	Mike Huckabee 8%
Secretary of Energy	Jeb Bush 5%
Secretary of Education	Ben Carson 13%
	Carly Fiorina 5%
	Mike Huckabee 4%
	Jeb Bush 4%
Secretary of Veteran's Affairs	Mike Huckabee 8%
	Lindsey Graham 6%
	Jeb Bush 5%
Secretary of Housing and Urban Development	Donald Trump 7%
	Ben Carson 4%
Department of the Interior	Jeb Bush 4%

The results above clearly show that voters have been paying attention to some of the debates! Lindsey Graham, for example, was perceived as having a strong performance regarding defense and foreign policy issues. Graham was identified as a potential Secretary of Defense or Secretary of Veteran's Affairs. Another candidate that has benefited from strong debate performance is Chris Christie. In the debates, Christie has mentioned his background as a prosecutor and his experience after 9/11 in developing standards for identifying terrorists. Christie scored highly as a potential Attorney General or Secretary of Homeland Security.

The backgrounds of the "outsiders", as well as strong debate performances by Carly Fiorina and Ben Carson, helped to identify them as potential Cabinet members in multiple categories. Fiorina, former CEO of Hewlett

Packard, was seen as a strong candidate for Secretary of Education, Secretary of Commerce, Secretary of the Treasury or even Secretary of State. Carson is viewed by many as the embodiment of the American Dream. He overcame an impoverished background to become a leading surgeon. As such, he has been identified as a potential Secretary of Health and Human Services, Secretary of Housing, Secretary of Urban Development, Secretary of Education, Secretary of the Treasury or even Secretary of State. Donald Trump was identified as a strong Secretary of Housing and Urban Development, Secretary of Homeland Security, Secretary of Commerce, or Secretary of the Treasury. Trump's experience in business and real estate probably influence voters in their perception of Trump's abilities to successfully fill these positions.

Additionally, it must be noted that Jeb Bush was the most frequently mentioned candidate to fill almost any of the Cabinet positions. Clearly voters respect Governor Bush's political experience and believe he could be an important part of any administration. In fact, Bush's father, President George H.W. Walker Bush, served within several administrations prior to becoming Vice President and ultimately President. Mike Huckabee was also mentioned in several of the categories, indicating that voters also hold respect for Governor Huckabee and believe he could complement a new administration.

Voters were supportive of the Republican Dream Team of 2016 concept. While each of the candidates believe that they can effectively do the job as President, it's important for the candidates to get their egos in check. If a candidate truly believes it is critical for a Republican to win the office of President in 2016, the candidates might want to reflect upon the most effective manner for the Party to win rather than just an individual candidate. Additionally, it is ultimately about fixing the administrative mess that currently represents our government. It would be hard to believe that many of these talented individuals would not be able to make a difference should they be appointed to some of these positions.

Voters will respond positively to candidates working together to win as a Team. Just as a sports team must work together to win a championship . . . not just relying on the talented quarterback in football or pitcher in baseball . . . voters would like to see those in government approach a problem with the ultimate goal of helping citizens rather than assuaging their own egos.

At the end of the book we have included a pledge in which we ask candidates to support the concept of working as a team rather than hurting the chances of the Republican Party. Do you think the candidates should take this pledge?

CHAPTER 12

THE INFLUENCERS

There are several "outsiders" that are not running for President but who influence Republican voters. Voters receive information about the election from various sources. These sources include the cable news channels, the traditional news channels, talk radio, blogs, various online sources as well as friends, family and local organizations. Religious organizations, as well as community groups, unions, national lobbying organizations and even book clubs, may provide information and recommendations. While the actual opinions of these individuals and groups are not included in this book (because they may vary as the race progresses), the amount of influence each of these organizations or individuals may have will be highlighted.

Focus group participants were asked where they received most of their information about the upcoming elections:

- 6 out of 10 indicated that they received information primarily from Fox News.
- All of the individuals indicated that they also listened to the network news.

- 3 out of 10 listen to both Fox and CNN so they feel they "get both sides of the story".
- 5 out of 10 listen to talk radio, primarily conservative talk radio, with one individual indicating he also listens to NPR sometimes.

Quantitative research with voters resulted in similar information sources.

- Fifty-two percent seek information from Fox News with that number increasing to 58 percent for those over the age of 65.
- Fifty-three percent indicated that they listen to the network news channels such as CBS, NBC and ABC for primary information.
- Forty-one percent of voters look primarily to their local news channels for information on elections.
- Thirty-eight percent of voters will look at online sources with 22 percent going to the candidate's websites.
- Thirty-four percent of voters turn to the national newspapers for information on the elections. Thirty-one percent read their local/regional newspaper.
- Twenty-nine percent will watch CNN for election information. PBS provides information to 14 percent of the voters who responded and 10 percent listen to NPR.
- Only 3 percent are watching Twitter feeds.

In addition to the information sources, voters were asked if there were specific individuals or organizations that they respected and that might influence their opinion.

While most voters were quick to reply that they make their own decisions, some of the following individuals and organizations were flagged as having some influence.

INDIVIDUAL OR ORGANIZATION	% VOTERS WHO INDICATE WILL OR MAY INFLUENCE THEIR VOTE
Bill O'Reilly	25%
Sean Hannity	18%
Charles Krauthammer	20%
Rush Limbaugh	15%
Sarah Palin	12%
Glenn Beck	14%
George W. Bush	29%
NRA (National Rifle Association)	23%
Union	4%
Neighbors	17%
Family members	43%
Local politicians	16%
Religious-based organizations	32%

Bill O'Reilly and Sean Hannity are well-known *Fox News* commentators. Both have a top-rated prime time nightly television show. Bill O'Reilly promotes a "balanced view" as his differentiator, while Hannity is perceived as being more conservative. A quarter of voters indicated they could be influenced by Bill O'Reilly's opinions on candidates. It's interesting to note that the percentages of voters indicating they would listen to Bill O'Reilly did not vary by age. Sean Hannity might influence 18 percent of voters, with older voters being somewhat more supportive of Hannity. Charles Krauthammer is an author and frequent and highly respected commentator on many of the *Fox News* shows. A fascinating result was that 34 percent of voters over age 65 would be influenced by Charles Krauthammer's opinions, compared to only 12% of those between the ages of 45–64 and 18% of those between the ages of 18–44. Clearly Mr. Krauthammer appeals to the older voters!

Glen Beck and Rush Limbaugh are conservative commentators as well. Rush Limbaugh, a National Radio Hall of Fame inductee, is well known for his daily radio show. Sarah Palin, former Vice-Presidential candidate in 2008 and former Governor of Alaska, is also an active commentator with multiple online publications, TV shows and an active social media presence. Rush Limbaugh was the most influential of these commentators. There were few differences among age groups regarding the influence of any of these individuals.

One of the most influential sources identified was former President George W. Bush. Twenty-nine percent of voters will be influenced by the former President's opinion of various candidates. It is interesting to note that this support did not vary by age. This will be important for candidates to keep in mind as the primaries progress. It can be assumed that President Bush will support his brother Jeb Bush in the primaries. If Jeb Bush is not able to garner enough support in the early primaries and is forced to drop out, it will be important for other candidates to seek the endorsement of the former President . . . if such an endorsement is available.

Family members, not surprisingly, were the most influential source at 43 percent. Older voters, those over age

65, were the least likely to be influenced by family members at 34 percent compared to younger voters, those ages 18–44, in which 58 percent acknowledged the influence of family members. Perhaps with age comes wisdom . . . or no longer caring what others think?

Seventeen percent of voters will listen to their neighbors. Local politicians influence sixteen percent and their unions' influence only 4 percent.

Twenty-three percent of voters indicated that the NRA would influence their vote. This same theme was echoed in the focus group. It's interesting to note that the NRA may influence 27 percent of voters between the ages of 18–44, 23 percent of voters in the 45–64 age group, and 20 percent of voters in the 65 plus group.

Finally, 32 percent of voters will be influenced by religious based organizations. This is the second highest category after Family members. This category was also highly influenced by age with the youngest voters most likely to be influenced by their religious based organization.

Capturing the support of voters is the primary goal of the candidates seeking the 2016 Presidential nomination. While the choice made by each voter is an individual decision, there are clearly organizations and individuals that influence many of these final decisions. The candidates need to convince not only the voter that they are the right candidate, but they also need to convince the influencers of their credentials. Who will be most successful influencing the influencers?

CHAPTER 13

REPUBLICAN DREAM TEAM 2016 TAKES THE STAGE

In a September 16, 2015 interview Megyn Kelly of Fox News asked Sean Spicer, Chief Strategist and Communications Director for Republican Party in Washington, about the large number of candidates running for president in the Republican Party. He responded, "It's not about the number. You look at the quality and diversity in this field. You're talking two Cuban-Americans; a world renowned black neurosurgeon; the first female Fortune 20 CEO; a successful businessman; former senators; former governors; current governors - these are amazing people!"

In fact, the original Republican field of seventeen candidates for President in 2016 is the largest presidential field in American history. Each candidate has a large base of constituents with common beliefs who support them. They have supporters from past elections at the local, state and national levels. They have wealthy donors and persons of influence on their team. Several have been tested as chief executives in the business world. In addition one is a physician who advanced science in separating conjoined twins while another is a well-known television celebrity who can astutely work the media.

> "... I'll continue to talk about issues. I just really don't buy into the attack-your-fellow-Republicans thing. I'm just not going to do that."
> —Ben Carson, CNN 10/24/15

The Republican Party speculates that Mitt Romney lost the presidential election of 2012 because of an extended and vitriol primary season. In fact the Republican Party has moved the Republican Convention from August to July to shorten the cycle. No one can disagree that the debates and jockeying for position in the polls has given the Democrats fodder for the eventual race against the Republican nominee. The candidates are left damaged in the eyes of the voters at large. Surely the Democrats were worried when they saw the formidable team of Republican candidates coming together at the October 28, 2015 debate against the CNBC moderators. The candidates' on point response to the poorly executed debate resonated not only with the studio audience but also with those of us watching at home.

CNBC debate moderator to the candidates: What's your weakness?

Chris Christie: There's not a lot of weakness on this stage.

Mike Huckabee: Trump would make a better candidate than Hillary—I fought the Clintons, beat them and lived to tell about it.

Marco Rubio: We have eleven good candidates—the Democrats can't come up with one!

Ted Cruz: How about talking about the substantive issues that people care about?

Frank Luntz, Fox News research commentator after 10/28/15 debate: Cruz' comment got a 98% from the focus group of conservatives and moderates and this is the first time during any focus group they erupted into cheers.

INTERCHANGE FOLLOWING 10/28/15 DEBATE:

"Candidates came to your defense."
—Sean Hannity, FOX News

"Certain camaraderie up there tonight—beautiful to watch"
—Donald Trump

Sadly, it took less than a week for some of the front-runners to detach themselves from the group as they tried to influence the format for future debates. The race back to the standard of divide and conquer was once again in full mode and the Democrats could once again relax knowing the Republicans would help their cause. It's the way things always have been done. Energy is wasted on looking at what's wrong with the candidates of their own party in order to win the primary election. We plant the seeds of running as a Dream Team before the first primary election in hopes it will germinate quickly before further damage is done to the Republican candidates. Is it possible for the candidates to return to the camaraderie they briefly enjoyed following the CNBC debate in October to unite under the Republican Dream Team Concept?

When you read the Republican candidates' stand on positions they generally agree on areas that desperately need fixing. They even mostly agree on "how" things need to be fixed (See Chapter 10). The conservative voter is right there with them in that agreement. What could happen if they began to work immediately as if they had already won the election? Working as a team they could begin to lay the foundation for a powerful platform for change. The Dream Team concept redirects the energy from disparaging whomever happens to be the day's front-runner in the polls, to staying focused on the issues and defeating the Democratic opponent. There is a riveting focus of the candidates, their teams and campaign funds on the strength of the team and getting them elected. With reporters finding it difficult to get negative news from within the Republican Party, they will find it hard not to focus on the innovative approach of the Republican Dream Team. The result is a positively aligned team, less damaged candidates and a team focused on working together to win the general election.

What else besides a fragmented Republican team with tattered candidates could happen if things continue on as they are? Instead of being a force to win, the wide field of candidates could create a vacuum when there is one winner and 16 losers following the primary election. As some candidates are forced out of the field by lack of funding and poor polling, discouraged republican and independent voters potentially lose enthusiasm for the November election. If instead their top pick is already a declared member of the Republican Dream Team of 2016, these same voters are more likely to continue to be engaged. The boots on the ground continue to walk, the dollars continue to flow and the voters remain committed because their candidate continues on as part of a team of candidates who are well positioned and qualified to lead the country.

"Idealistic? Absolutely—can still change the world—stronger families, know our neighbors, come together as a country—great from the bottom up... renew America if we work together"
—John Kasich, CNBC Debate, 10-28-15

Some voters will like the idea of a Dream Team because they are weary of politics as usual and will embrace a new promising idea out of disillusionment over the existing system. However, there will also be voters who are opposed to any change regardless of how positively it is positioned. They would rather stick with the "tried and true" approach rather than risk making a mistake. Having more people on the team can be a reassuring thing especially if the group were viewed as trustworthy. When investing in a company, people often look at the leadership team in making their decisions. Knowing the entire team might give a voter more confidence and maintain them as invested voters. Since individual candidates find it difficult to fulfill every voters needs, a team of candidates can come closer to having all the "boxes checked" on experience and issues that are important to an individual voter or groups of voters. However, if a person's choice for president decides not to become part of the dream team or if that voter has a dislike for one of the members of the dream team—that missing team member or dislike of one of the team members could have a contagion affect and lead the voter to denounce the entire team. Sometimes an individual checked box could turn off voters as well as recruit them.

The Dream Team approach is not too far of a departure from the current process. Each candidate would be slotted for at least two key cabinet positions. The Vice President could be the person with the second most votes in the Republican primary. When the candidate for president and vice president are selected, the remainder of the team would move into their designated cabinet slots. The team is still "appointed" based on capability—it's just more transparent to the voter at the time of the general election. With a Republican Dream Team, instead of worrying about the complexity of a wide range of candidates, voters can refocus, be less vigilant and reassured that the team is already identified and establishing the platform of needed changes.

The natural response for a candidate who is forced to drop out or does not win a race is to withdraw for a bit, lick their wounds and rest while they decide what's next. Many hope to resurrect their momentum for another run at a future date. Under the Dream Team concept there would be no time for stepping back. Each member of the team will know exactly what posts on the cabinet they will most likely lead when the Republicans successfully win the general election. Their role is to immediately help the republican candidates for president and vice president win the general election. Without missing a beat, they remain on the campaign trail promoting the benefits of a "winning team" to accomplish all the things discussed during the presidential primary. What could happen if they began to work immediately as if they had already won the election? Working as a team they could begin to lay the foundation for a powerful platform for change. They also begin to naturally coalesce to find every opportunity to prepare as a team for the actions they take beginning January 21, 2017.

So why would candidates buy into this concept of running as the Republican Dream Team? First and foremost, based on their statements, you would think they would want a Republican candidate to be elected. If not them, surely they would want another person with conservative credentials to be president. They have all stressed the dire situation of our country. They have all affirmed their love for our country. They have all pledged to "fix" what is wrong and move the United States of America into a positive future. They have all committed to putting their current careers and lives on hold for at least four years to allow them to focus on accomplishing the work of "righting" the country. All of the candidates would still be at the seat of power. Instead of the coordinating function of the president, they each would lead a very sizeable organization with up to $1.2 trillion in allocations (HHS) and over 3.2 million federal employees (Department of Defense). Anyone of the cabinet posts from the viewpoint of the budget, number of employees and systemic problems is a sizable undertaking that demands qualified/vetted leadership. For purely pragmatic reasons a successful record of turning around the bureaucracy of one behemoth federal organization would be a great platform for a future run for the office of president. The combined efforts of so many gifted people has to be a more powerful way of achieving the Republican agenda then the typical political cabinet appointments made by the president after the election.

Part of the preparation for their run as president involves understanding all the workings of the executive branch, including the cabinet positions. Each candidate would be positioned to work successfully with other cabinet members through that shared understanding of all the positions. Imagine the conversations of this Republican Dream Team Cabinet. One cabinet member puts forth an idea. The governors in the group would explain the impact of such a decision at the state level and whether the federal government or the State should lead. The Senators would justify why federal leadership is needed and explain what it would take to move the idea through Congress and begin to formulate a plan to work their relationships in both houses toward a positive vote. The business leaders and professionals would explain the impact to corporations and the creation of jobs. One of them might even begin to question why the government at any level should be involved instead of letting the free market lead.

With each scenario you would have a group of powerful people, not president pleasers, who would speak their mind and come to agreement. The natural tension between the voices makes for wise decisions and positions the concept to gain the support of all levels of government, business leaders and the American people as a whole. For individual issues, such as the best team to work with a particular foreign leader, the team decides which mix of relationships, personal attributes and expertise makes the most sense. Each day the agenda, intentional plan for success and the role of the individual players is implemented in a strategic manner.

Why wouldn't the candidates and their campaign teams want to band together to move the country in a more conservative and positive direction? Ego and power. Can we agree that anyone who is a candidate for President of the United States possesses a fairly healthy ego? So what would cause a confident candidate for president to pledge to be part of a "Republican Dream Team?" Perhaps they would realize the Dream Team gives the US Government and the American people the best shot of changing the direction of this large, lumbering centralized government that is moving rapidly away from fundamental vision of a limited government and a people who are free. Those who have power under the current system, like campaign managers and big donors, might not welcome the change. They might fear losing the power they currently hold in the old system. It will take the abandoning of ego of the individual candidates and of the power of campaign teams and donors in favor of bringing our best political minds to a common table for the good of the country. Candidates have already taken a pledge not to run as an "independent" should they lose the primary. What if the candidates also align under a pledge to continue on as part of the executive team should they not win the Republican primary and/or pledge to appoint their former opponents as part of their leadership team if they win? (See Appendix A).

Can you see in your minds eye a line of confident, talented leaders walking side by side across the White House lawn . . . a real force to be reckoned with, an impossible team to beat and the country turned around more quickly than could ever be imagined? The new bold idea could energize the country as much as a moon walk and inspire the world with what is possible in a free society. Putting the dream above everything else, as our forefathers did, focuses The Republican Dream Team of 2016 for the massive job ahead . . . and brings hope to freedom loving people everywhere.

"I bring greetings from the wonderful guy who is still very proud to have been Ronald Reagan's vice president. A competition turned into friendship, and the better my Dad got to know Ronald Reagan, the more he admired and loved him."
—Jeb Bush, Jeb2016.com

CHAPTER 14

WHAT'S AT STAKE?

Many agree there are significant ways in which our federal government could improve. The October Quinnipiac poll found 71 percent of citizens are unhappy with the direction our country is going. Ann Romney put it more simply in an interview on Fox News Sunday (10/1/15) when she stated, "People want a leader to come in with a wrecking ball." Whether it is reducing the ever increasing debt level, the failure to adequately care for our veterans or the insolvency of our Medicare/Medicaid programs, there is a need for improvement not only in the services provided by the federal government but with how the branches of government are functioning-can you say gridlock?

In an increasingly complex world where information on every candidate is easily available with a little research on the web, voters are less likely to just accept what is printed on the candidate's campaign literature, stated on their website, or presented in a speech. Therefore, it becomes increasingly difficult to find a candidate who does not have some liability in his or her resume for every voter.

The constant buzz of information can make someone a "news junkie" or turn people away from the political process for less stressful forms of entertainment. What is at stake is finding a way to educate voters on the candidates without overwhelming them—to keep them involved without discouraging them. The political process in many ways has become a reality show. Although entertaining, the depth of engagement is lacking for many citizens.

The American people need to see some real positive movement on the issues that gravely concern them. With people like Vladimir Putin openly touting the benefits of a dictator as a response to weak leadership in democracies, it would be naïve to think that our continued method of government is not threatened. The Tea Party movement sends legislator after legislator to the federal level only to be disappointed that the legislation they want blocked is passed and the legislation they want passed is thwarted. System theory tells us that when you have good people who continue to fail within a system the problem may not be with the people-the problem may be with the system.

Think about opening day of the Olympics. As the countries parade into the main arena you can begin to speculate which country is entering under their flag by the appearance of the team. Now think about when the U.S. team enters the arena. The U.S. Team certainly looks like a mixture of all of the other countries. We are different not because of how we look—we are different because of our founding beliefs about government. In 2008 one of the authors was told by an executive in a major corporation who was an immigrant from India "The people of India are not mad at the United States because of the Iraq War. They are mad at the United States because all of our lives we looked at America and said to ourselves 'America is where they get government right.' And when the Americans mess up their government they mess up democracy for the whole world."

The foundational system is not the problem. Not holding true to a limited federal government is the problem. Can we peel back the layers of "intrusion", "procedure" and "complexity" that have been added to how our government operates? Can we change the course on how we do the work of government so our ability to sprint and thrive is revived? The process for creating legislation by design moves intentionally through our system to make certain the right checks and balances are in place. However, how that system currently functions is not slow by intended design but rather by gamesmanship focused on winning instead of arriving at a balanced solution. This fast-paced, dynamic world in which we find ourselves requires our system to be nimble, lean and able to sprint to continue to thrive. Special interests and trying to do too much for too many people from the federal level is bogging us down. The authors wonder if we can prevent messing up democracy for the whole world? Can we prevent messing it up for ourselves?

Candidates who have experience in state and federal government in cooperation with people who have functioned at the highest levels of our corporate and medical systems surely can begin the work of digging the United States out of the quagmire in which we currently find ourselves. It will be a battle. All 17 of the Republican candidates are battle-tested. Many who benefit from the current system through power, entitlements or other "false prophets of democracy" will not want to see the system changed. They know the old games and they are good at them. They profit from them through power, wealth and special privilege whether through influence or entitlements. They've worked hard to become competent in the system that has become so fractured that it hardly aligns any longer with the original intent and dreams of our founding fathers. It is a house of cards that needs a strong team with the courage to peel off the weight of ineffective layers of government that have been piled onto a simple system that once allowed us to live as a free people. Government cannot make us free. More government does just the opposite. Those who drafted the Constitution understood this and we, the American people, appear to have forgotten it.

There's an old lore about an early member of the US House of Representatives returning to his community on horseback. One of his fellow federal legislators had died in office recently and the Congress voted to give his widow a stipend. As he was visiting with his neighbor and telling him the unfortunate story of the legislator's death and the caring generosity of the Congress, the neighbor responded sharply, "It was not your money to give!" Is that not the crux of the problem? Our Founding Fathers did not intend for the federal government to fix every ill no matter how good the cause. Instead they intended the federal government to do specific things and to do them well. Even though they left implementation up to the future, do you believe the Founding Fathers that fought against the tyranny of England intended the federal government to develop into the large bureaucracy it is today?

In reality, the further the entity trying to solve the problem is away from the problem, both in distance and experience, the less effective the solution. There is deeply embedded context within every community that is understood at a visceral level. Without the history, context and ownership the solution will be less effective, the implementation faulty, less successful, short-lived . . . and more expensive. With each leg of the journey the money travels to a centralized government, it decreases in value as more hands are paid to touch the money, there is less personal accountability and the chance for graft and corruption increases. Putin looking in at our ineffective democracy is touting that a dictatorship is "the way to go." People who are discouraged, anxious and pre-occupied may just begin to sigh and say, "Maybe Putin is right—with a benevolent dictator life would be easier and less messy." In fact, is that not we have done in many ways? We send our money to Washington trusting they will bring the best minds to solve the problems we face, dust off our hands and get on with our lives.

It has been said that a frog put into a pot of water on the stove with the heat gradually increasing will slowly cook to death without jumping out of the pot. After a hard day at work, taking care of the family and trying to make ends meet . . . we "unplug" from the complexity of the current world, engage in mass interaction on a surface level (can you say "Facebook"?) and fail to really talk in depth to no one. Those who won our liberty, talked deeply about the fundamental principles and structure of the federal government "for the people and by the people" and questioned whether that government could "long endure." Our enemies are looking in and betting "not." So why did our ancestors fight and die in the revolution? Why do millions of people try to come to this country legally or illegally? Because we are a "free people"—well, at least we are for now.

APPENDIX A

DREAM TEAM PLEDGE

Below is a sample pledge that each candidate who endorses "The Republican Dream Team" concept could take. The authors modeled the pledge after the pledge each candidate has already signed pledging not to run as a third party candidate. The authors see this pledge as a litmus test of how committed the candidates are to serving our country during these difficult and dangerous times in our history.

"I [name] affirm that if I win the 2016 Republican nomination for President, I will select my Vice Presidential running mate and cabinet members from the slate of candidates running for the Republican nomination for President. I further pledge that I will run my campaign for President in such a manner not to alienate these candidates from myself and the voters thereby precluding them and their constituents from wanting to join my team in leading our country into a positive future."

APPENDIX B

VOTER WORKSHEET

Use the Voter Worksheet on the next page to make your "Republican Dream Team" selections. In keeping with the Republican Dream Team concept, all seventeen original candidates for the Republican nomination are included below. As you make your selections, review the available positions (Chapter 3), the candidates' backgrounds and stand on issues most important to you (Chapter 5, 6, 7, 10, and Appendix C).

- Step 1: Mark the candidates still in the race for the Republican Nomination in Column 2 with an "X"
- Step 2: Read Chapter 3 again on the role of President, Vice President
- Step 3: Write a list of experience, personal leadership traits and issues that are important to you.
- Step 4: Select your choice for President from those who are still in the race.
- Step 5: Select your choice for Vice President.
- Step 6: Read Chapter 3 again on the Cabinet Positions.
- Step 7: Select your choice for each of the fifteen Cabinet Positions

The Republican Dream Team of 2016

CANDIDATE	X	POSITION ON DREAM TEAM
Jeb Bush		
Ben Carson		
Chris Christie		
Ted Cruz		
Carly Fiorina		
Jim Gilmore		
Lindsey Graham		
Mike Huckabee		
Bobby Jindal		
John Kasich		
Rand Paul		
George Pataki		
Rick Perry		
Marco Rubio		
Rick Santorum		
Donald Trump		
Scott Walker		

APPENDIX C

OVERVIEW OF CANDIDATES

Jeb Bush Summary Chart

JEB BUSH	Background
	Born 1953
Marital Status and Children	Columba Garnica Gallo (1974–Present)
	3 children
	4 grandchildren
Religious Affiliation	Roman Catholic
Education	University of Texas, Austin, Latin American Studies (1973)
Work Experience	Texas Commerce Bank, branch manager, Vice President (1974–1980)
	Codina Group (1980–1986)
Political Experience	Dade County Republican Party, Chairman (1985)
	Florida Secretary of Commerce (1986–1988)
	Campaign manager (1989)
	Candidate for Florida Governor (1994)
	George H.W. Bush campaign volunteer (1980 and 1988)
	Governor of Florida (1998–2006)

Continued

JEB BUSH	Background
Other Experience	Established Points of Light Program (2000)
	Volunteered for Miami Children's Hospital and Dade County Homeless Trust and United Way (1994–1998)
Relevant Publications	*Profiles in Character* (1996)
	Reply All (2015)
	Immigration Wars: Forging an American Solution (2013)

Sources: www.jeb2016.com, www.wikipedia.com

JEB BUSH	Recap of Issues
Economy	Proposes Reform and Growth Act of 2017 which will lower taxes, eliminate loopholes in the tax code and lower corporate tax rate
	Will submit a Balanced Budget Amendment to control and eliminate the National Debt
	Place a freeze on federal hiring with a 1:3 rule that allows one new hire for three employees who leave
	Line item veto for President
	Approve energy development i.e. The Keystone Pipeline (or similar)
	Repeal or reform Dodd-Frank, Waters of the U.S. Rule, Carbon Rule, Coal Ash Rule
	Supports net neutrality
Taxes	Three personal tax brackets: 28%, 25%, and 10%. No tax for those who make less than $15,000
	Corporate tax rate: 20%
	Expand earned income tax credit, eliminate marriage penalty, alternative minimum tax and death tax
	Eliminate payroll tax for those over age 62

Continued

JEB BUSH	Recap of Issues
Immigration	Secure the border
	Require individuals to pass a thorough background check, pay fines, learn English
	Supports a provisional work permit that allows a person who actually works and does not receive government assistance over an extended time to earn legal status
	Use new technology to achieve continuous surveillance of the border and increase flexibility of Border Patrol
	Send home those who overstay their visas
	Crack down on sanctuary cities
Foreign Policy/ National Security/ Terrorism	Support Iraqi forces as they rebuild their security and support Sunni tribes to break free of Iranian influence
	Give Kurds weapons and other power to defeat ISIS
	Support moderates in Syria and improve recruitment and training of forces to fight ISIS
	Work with Allies and declare a no-fly zone
	Public and private sectors should work together to protect against government hacking
	Restore funding to intelligence community, Defense Department and FBI to protect against cyber hacking; develop agreements with Allies around the world; hold those who steal our nation's intellectual capital accountable
Entitlements	Repeal Obamacare

Sources: www.jeb206.com, www.wikipedia.com

Ben Carson Summary Chart

BEN CARSON	Background
	Born 1951
Marital Status and Children	Lacena ("Candy) Rustin (1975–Present)
	3 children
Religion	Seventh Day Adventist
Education	John Hopkins Hospital, Residency in Neurosurgery
	University of Michigan, M.D. (1977)
	Yale University, B.A., (1973)
Work Experience	Director of Pediatric Neurosurgery. John Hopkins Hospital, (1984–2013)
	First to separate conjoined twins, (1983)
	Washington Times, weekly opinion columnist (2013–2014)
	Fox News commentator
Additional Information	2001 Library of Congress Living Legend
	2008 Presidential Medal of Freedom
	2010 National Academy of Sciences Institute of Medicine
	2014, Gallup Organization, No. 6 on list of World's Most Admired Men
Relevant Publications	*Gifted Hands: The Ben Carson Story* (1992)
	America the Beautiful: Rediscovering What Made This Nation Great (2013)
	One Nation: What We Can All Do to Save America's Future (2014)
	One Vote: Make Your Voice Heard (2014)
	A More Perfect Union: What We the People Can Do to Reclaim Our Constitutional Liberties (2015)

Sources: www.bencarson.com, www.wikipedia.com

BEN CARSON	Recap of Issues
Economy	Ratify a Balanced Budget Amendment to the Constitution. Minimum wage should probably be raised and then indexed (www.ontheissues.org) Sep 2015
Taxes	Supports a flat tax of 10%: no deductions; rebate for people at the poverty level (FBN 10/10/15) Wants wholesale tax reform: fairer, simpler, more equitable tax system End IRS as we know it Forms should be simpler and easy to complete
Immigration	We have the ability to build a border wall but not the will (www.ontheissues.org) Sep 2015
Foreign Policy/ National Defense/ Terrorism	Stand by Israel ISIS: Syrian refugees should stay in Jordan and we should provide aggressive funding to care for them (*Newsmax*, 11/29/2015) Global Jihadists "goal is to destroy us and our way of life. We must engage in a war of ideas against the radicals abroad. Putting the special ops there to guide some of the other things we are doing there...We have to destroy their Caliphate—will make them look like losers and that will lessen their influence." *Fox News* Republican Debate Nov 2015 Aggressiveness of Russia is a threat to peace and security Must lead Allies, both NATO and non-NATO from a place of strength
Entitlements	Obamacare is a "monstrosity": supports Health Savings Accounts that allow families to make their own decisions and drive down health care costs Get rid of dependency. That is true compassion. (www.ontheissues.org) Feb 2015
Social Issues	Second Amendment: Second Amendment rights are fundamental Abortion: Pro-life

Sources: www.bencarson.com, www.wikipedia.com

Chris Christie Summary Chart

CHRIS CHRISTIE	Background
	Born 1962
Marital Status and Children	Mary Pat Foster (1985–Present)
	4 children
Religious Affiliation	Roman Catholic
Education	University of Delaware, B.A. Political Science (1984)
	Seton Hall University, School of Law, J.D. (1987)
Work Experience	Dughi, Hewit, & Palatuca, (Lawyer and Lobbyist (1987–2001); Partner (1993)
Political Experience	Morris County Board (1994–1998)
	Candidate for NJ Assembly (1995), unsuccessful
	Appointed U.S. Attorney (2001–2008)
	Governor of New Jersey (2009–Present)
Other Experience	
Relevant Publications	

Sources: www.chrischristie.com, www.wikipedia.com

OVERVIEW OF CANDIDATES

CHRIS CHRISTIE

	Recap of Issues
Economy	Control Regulations Revoke any Executive Orders from present administration on the first day "Regulatory Zero": For each new regulation imposed, one of equal cost must be removed Impose hard cap on what it can cost employer to comply with federal regulations Reduce costs for both employer and employee of creating jobs and working Eliminate payroll taxes for those over age 62 and those under age 25 Lift ban on crude oil exports Invest in technology
Taxes	
Immigration	Secure border: build a wall where appropriate (urbanized areas); increase manpower; and use advanced technology (drones, electronic surveillance) Universal workplace enforcement; every employer must use E-Verify Track overstay of visas with biometric technology Eliminate funding for sanctuary cities
National Security/ Foreign Policy/ Terrorism	Absolute commitment to Israel Strengthen alliances across Asia-Pacific Stand with Western Alliance against Russian aggression Confront ISIS and check Iran through regional coalitions Stand with Allies Encourage NATO to invest more in their own defense Build offensive cyber warfare capabilities; strike back when necessary

Continued

CHRIS CHRISTIE	Recap of Issues
Entitlements	Repeal Obamacare's 30 hour work week mandate Social Security: reduce benefits for wealthier individuals; future retirees with income of $80,000 per year (outside of Social Security) will receive full benefits; those with outside income exceeding $80,000 will receive benefits on a sliding scale; those with more than $200,000 of outside income will receive no benefits; the amounts will be higher for couples; raise normal retirement age to 69; implement gradually beginning in 2022; one time 5 percent increase in benefits for all beneficiaries when they reach 85

Sources: www.ChrisChristie.com, www.wikipedia.com

Ted Cruz Summary Chart

RAFAEL EDWARD "TED" CRUZ	Background
	Born 1970
Marital Status and Children	Heidi Nelson (2001–present) 2 children
Religious Affiliation	Baptist
Education	Princeton University, B.A., Public Policy (1992) Harvard Law School, J.D., magna cum laude, (1995)
Work Experience	Cooper and Kirk, L.L.C., Attorney (1997–1998) University of Texas School of Law, Adjunct Professor (2004–2009) Morgan, Lewis & Bockius, L.L.P. Attorney (2008–2013)
Political Experience	U.S. Court of Appeals, Law Clerk (1995) U.S. Supreme Court, Chief Justice William Rehnquist, Law Clerk (1996) Office of Policy Planning, Federal Trade Commission, Director (1999–2003) George W. Bush, Domestic Policy Adviser (1999) U.S. Department of Justice, Associate Deputy Attorney General (2000) Texas Solicitor General (2003–2008) U.S. Senator (2013–Present)
Other Experience	Named "Conservative of the Year" by multiple conservative organizations
Relevant Publications	*A Time for Truth: Reigniting the Promise of America* (2015)

Sources: www.tedcruz.org, www.wikipedia.com

TED CRUZ	Recap of Issues
Economy	Abolish four unnecessary Cabinet agencies and the IRS
	Eliminate 25 Agencies, Bureaus and Commissions, known as the Federal "ABCs"
	Amend the Constitution to require a balanced budget
	Federal hiring freeze: institute freeze on hiring of federal civilian employees and reform automatic worker raises
	Prevent internet from becoming public utility to spur innovation and entrepreneurship
	Remove federal impediments to energy exploration
	Opposes Renewable Fuel Standard ethanol subsidy and opposes moratorium on offshore exploration in Gulf of Mexico
Taxes	Create flat tax of 10%: no taxes for families who make less than $36,000 annually
	Business Flat Tax of 16%
	Get rid of the IRS
	Be able to file taxes via cell phone
Immigration	Triple size of U.S. Border patrol
	Complete the wall
	End sanctuary cities
	Wants to streamline immigration system: segment visas, create real and transparent caps by country; eliminate the diversity requirements
	Prevent illegal aliens from receiving benefits
	End birthright citizenship

Continued

TED CRUZ	Recap of Issues
National Security/ Foreign Policy/ Terrorism	All military efforts should have explicit objective and be directly linked to U.S. security-get out when objective is reached
	ISIS: Authored Act that would prevent Americans who join ISIS from returning to U.S.
	"Acknowledge 'the evil' of 'radical Islamic terrorism'; 'we are at war with the Islamic State' "Unless the U.S. acts to defeat terrorism, 'this violence will come to America'"; "The Kurds are our boots on the ground." MSNBC interview, 11/14/15
	Pressured U.S. to lift unprecedented FAA ban on flights to Israel
	Led legislation to provide rewards for information leading to arrest of Hamas terrorists
Entitlements	Strike down Medicare Prescription Act Drug program as violation of States' Rights
	Repeal Obamacare
Social Issues	Second Amendment: authored legislation to prevent restrictions against Second Amendment rights
	Abortion: ban Partial Birth Abortion; supports parental notification and the Texas laws that prohibit state funds for groups that provide abortion
	Marriage: states should have the right to define marriage; wants to pass constitutional amendment

Sources: www.TedCruz.org, www.wikipedia.com

Carly Fiorina Summary Chart

CARLY FIORINA	Background
	Born 1954
Marital Status and Children	Todd Bartlem (1977–1984)
	Frank Fioriana (1985–Present)
	2 stepchildren
Religion	Christian Non-denominational
	Raised Episcopalian
Education	MIT Sloan School of Management, M.S. (1989)
	University of Maryland, Robert H. Smith School of Business, M.B.A., Marketing (1980)
	Stanford University, B.A., Medieval History and Philosophy (1976)
Work History	AT&T
	Management Trainee (1980)
	SVP, Corporate Equipment and Technology (1990)
	Spinoff of Lucent Technologies from AT&T, led Corporate Operations
	Planned 1996 IPO of Lucent Technologies, most successful IPO to have occurred at that time
	Lucent Technologies, President of Consumer Products (1996–1999)
	Hewlett Packard, CEO (1999–2005)
	Fox News, Commentator (2007)

Continued

CARLY FIORINA	Background
Political Experience	Republican National Committee Fundraising Chairman, 2008 Defense Business Board CIA External Advisory Board (2007–2009) Candidate for U.S. Senate, California (2010)
Other Experience	Chairman, Good360-donates merchandise to charities (2012) The One Woman Initiative-supports organizations in Muslim countries that provide empowerment to women
Relevant Publications	*Tough Choices: A Memoir* (2007) *Rising to the Challenge: My Leadership Journey* (2015)

Sources: www.carlyforpresident.com, www.wikipedia.com

CARLY FIORINA	Recap of Issues
Economy	Engine of economy is small business: must decrease regulation to support business
	Reform Fannie May, Freddie Mac
	Repeal Dodd-Frank
	Implement zero-based budgeting
	Take money from military bureaucracy and invest in front line
	Do not replace Baby Boomer government workers as they retire
	Insert meritocracy into federal government
	Provide training through local collaborations, not federal government
	Supports free trade
	Has conducted business in 170 countries
Taxes	Lower rates
	Reduce tax code to three pages
Immigration	Supports Dream Act because not fair to punish children
	Create visa validation system to make sure that individuals actually go home
	Not only are illegal immigrants crossing the border but so are drug lords and potentially terrorists
	Must secure the border and enforce existing laws
	Need to have path to legal status but not citizenship

Continued

OVERVIEW OF CANDIDATES 175

CARLY FIORINA	Recap of Issues
National Security/ Foreign Policy/ Terrorism	Cannot let Syrian refugees into the country until we have a process in place to vet these people *Washington Examiner*, 11/16/15
	"It enrages me." In response to Obama's comment that he wasn't interested in "pursuing some notion of American leadership" after terrorist activities in Paris *Interview with radio host, Hugh Hewitt*.
	Character of our nation needs to be protected
	Must require true inspections in Iran
	Need to push back at Putin: rebuild sixth fleet and missile defense program in Poland; ramp up troop presence in Germany
	China is in violation of international agreements by construction of islands in South China Sea: block trade routes; show by actions, not words, that this is unacceptable
Entitlements	Government must effectively execute and clean up the mess
	Obamacare is too complicated: must let states manage high-risk pools; create a competitive health care marketplace
Social Issues	Marriage: supports civil unions but marriage has a spiritual foundation and should only be man and woman; should not distribute benefits unequally
	Abortion: pro-life; no abortions after five months

Sources: www.carlyforpresident.com, www.wikipedia.com

Jim Gilmore Summary Chart

JAMES STUART "JIM" GILMORE	Background
	Born 1949
Marital Status and Children	Roxanne Gatling (1977–Present)
	2 children
Religious Affiliation	Methodist
Education	University of Virginia, B.A. (1971), J.D. (1977)
Work Experience	U.S. Army Intelligence (1971–1974)
Political Experience	Commonwealth Attorney (1987–1993)
	Attorney General of Virginia (1993–1997)
	Governor of Virginia (1998–2002)
	Chairman of RNC (2001–2002)
	Presidential candidate (2007)
	Senate campaign (2008)
Other Experience	Gilmore Commission, Chaired the Congressional Advisory Panel: Domestic Capabilities for Terrorism Involving Weapons of Mass Destruction (1999–2003)
	Chairman of RNC (2001–2002)
Relevant Publications	

Sources: www.gilmoreforamerica.com, www.wikipedia.com

OVERVIEW OF CANDIDATES 177

JIM GILMORE	Recap of Issues
Economy	See Growth for America Code
Taxes	Simplify tax code: progressive tax of 10%, 15%, or 25%; no double taxation
	Unified tax form for businesses: 15% tax for business-created income; deduct expenses immediately; repatriate profits earned abroad tax-free
	Continue mortgage deductions, charitable contributions
	Every citizen pays some form of tax: tax credits for families making less than poverty level
Immigration	Secure borders
	No sanctuary cities
	No amnesty: if came here illegally should never be eligible for citizenship
	Develop path to citizenship for immigrants that work hard, pay taxes, learn to speak English
National Security/ Foreign Policy/ Terrorism	Create Middle Eastern alliance similar to NATO
	Increase and strengthen intelligence capabilities
	Support moderate Muslim leaders
Entitlements	Replace Obamacare with patient-oriented healthcare system: maintain ability of young to remain on parents' policies until age 26; cover pre-existing conditions; interstate sale of insurance; promote Association Health Plans and Health Savings Accounts; allow income-adjusted, "advanceable" and refundable health insurance premium credits; tax deductions for income spent on health insurance; malpractice and provider antitrust reform
Social Issues	Second Amendment: every state and DC must honor concealed carry weapons permits; no ban on assault weapons.
	Global warming: U.S. cannot solve alone

Sources: www.gilmoreforamerica.com, www.wikipedia.com

Lindsey Graham Summary Chart

LINDSEY GRAHAM	Background
	Born 1955
Marital Status and Children	Single
	No children
	Adopted sister upon death of parents
Religious Affiliation	Baptist
Education	University of South Carolina, B.A. Psychology (1977)
	University of South Carolina, School of Law, J.D. (1981)
Work Experience	U.S. Air Force (1982–1988)
	Private Practice, Lawyer
Political Experience	South Carolina House of Representatives (1991–1994)
	U.S. House of Representatives (1994–2002)
	U.S. Senate (2002–Present)
	Committee on Armed Services
	Committee on the Judiciary
	Committee on Education and the Workforce
	Committee on International Relations
	Gang of 14
Other Experience	South Carolina National Guard, Guardsmen First
	Air Force Reserves, Colonel
Relevant Publications	*My Story* (2015)

Sources: www.lindseygraham.com, www.wikipedia.com

OVERVIEW OF CANDIDATES 179

LINDSEY GRAHAM	Recap of Issues
Economy	Supports Balanced Budget amendment
	Introduce "sunset provisions"; build in a process to review regulations, their cost-effectiveness and ensure accountability
	Streamline regulations
Taxes	Lower marginal rates for both individuals and corporations
Immigration	Hire, train and deploy new Border Patrol agents and complete the border fence
	Make E-verify mandatory
	Employ Entry-Exit system at all air and sea ports of entry for U.S.
	Force illegal immigrants to live under our rules not theirs
	Status quo is the same as amnesty
	Make illegal immigrants pay steep fines, register with the government, pay taxes, learn English and get in line behind all legal immigrants seeking citizenship
	Rescind Executive Orders

Continued

LINDSEY GRAHAM	Recap of Issues
National Security/ Foreign Policy/ Terrorism	Provide aid to those fighting back against ISIS
	Combine diplomacy, strong military and economic development tools to fight off radicalism around the globe
	End across the board military cuts
	Support military families and veterans
	Make sound military decisions
	Provide a clearly articulated and unified strategy
	Repair and reaffirm our relationship with Israel
	Re-engage with Allies
	Will need at least 10,000 troops deployed in the region to defeat ISIS
	Work closely with the Kurds to train and equip
	Create no-fly zones
	Aggressively apply air power
	Expand intelligence capabilities
	Fully utilize special ops.
Entitlements	Repeal Obamacare immediately: implement workable reforms; allow small businesses to form association health plans to pool risk and keep cost down
	Social Security: gradually increase the retirement age; begin means testing; hold those already in retirement harmless
	Eliminate waste and fraud in existing programs

Continued

LINDSEY GRAHAM	Recap of Issues
Social Issues	Second Amendment: stop the assault weapon ban; stand firm against the UN Arms Trade Treaty; UN should have no say on our Second Amendment rights
	Marriage: defends traditional marriage and believes the states have the right to determine their own marriage laws; respects the Supreme Court's decision and does not believe that a Constitutional Amendment would ever be supported
	Abortion: prevent taxpayer funding of abortions; enact Graham 20-Week Pain Capable Unborn Child Protection Act

Sources: www.lindseygraham.com, www.wikipedia.com

Mike Huckabee Summary Chart

MIKE HUCKABEE	Background
	Born 1955
Marital Status and Children	Janet McCain (1974–Present))
	3 children
	5 grandchildren
Religious Affiliation	Baptist
Education	Ouachita Baptist University, B.A. Religion, magna cum laude
	Southwestern Baptist Theological Seminary, did not graduate
Work Experience	Televangelist, Staff (1976–1980)
	Immanuel Baptist Church, Pine Bluff, Arkansas, Pastor (1980–1986)
	Beech Street Baptist Church, Texarkana, Arkansas, Pastor (1986–1992)
	Arkansas Baptist Convention, President (1989–1991)
	The Huckabee Report radio show (2009–2015)
	Fox News, Huckabee Show (2008–2015)
Political Experience	Lieutenant Governor of Arkansas, (1993–1996)
	Governor of Arkansas (1996–2007)
	Presidential Candidate (2008)
Other Experience	
Relevant Publications	*Do the Right Thing: Inside the Movement That is Bringing Common Sense Back to America* (2008)
	God, Guns, Grits and Gravy (2015)
	A Simple Government: Twelve Things We Really Need from Washington (and a Trillion We Don't) (2011)
	From Hope to Higher Ground: 12 Steps to Restoring America's Greatness (2007)
	Numerous additional publications

Sources: www.mikehuckabee.com, www.wikipedia.com

OVERVIEW OF CANDIDATES

MIKE HUCKABEE	Recap of Issues
Economy	Supports energy independence: explore all forms of domestically produced energy (oil, gas, wind, solar, bio-fuels, hydroelectric, nuclear, coal); supports a pipeline, such as the Keystone Pipeline; explore outer continental shelf
Taxes	Abolish the IRS Establish a Fair Tax: take all corporate taxes and replace with consumption tax for those above poverty level; Progressive Tax: tax collected at retail level
Immigration	Reject Obama's Executive Orders Secure border with a fence Increase border personnel Increase visas for those who legally enter the country Make illegal immigrants register and return to home country within 120 days: failing to do so would carry a 10-year ban on re-entering country
National Defense/ Foreign Policy/ Terrorism	Free trade must be fair trade: opposes TPP Supports economic sanctions against China Rebuild America's military superiority: avoid conflict by building a lethal fighting force Keep all options on the table when dealing with Radical Islam Stand with the Jewish people Stop Iran nuclear deal Do not allow Russia to annex Ukraine and Georgia: work with Allies Emphasize cyber-warfare capabilities: hack the Chinese government; hack individual cellphones of Communist Chinese leaders; wipe out their computer systems; retaliate proportionately when U.S. is hacked

Continued

MIKE HUCKABEE	Recap of Issues
Entitlements	Aggressively prosecute Medicare fraud
	Make sure everyone is paying into the Social Security system
	Repeal Obamacare
	New plan should allow for pre-existing conditions
Social Issues	Second Amendment: opposes new gun laws; protect rights of gun owners
	Marriage: supports traditional marriage
	Abortion: opposes public funding of abortions; supports parental notification
	Supports Scout Rule on Global Warming: "Leave the earth better than we found it."

Sources: *www.mikehuckabee.com, www.wikipedia.com*

John Kasich Summary Chart

JOHN KASICH	Background
	Born 1952
Marital Status and Children	Karen Waldbillig (1997–Present)
	Mary Lee Griffith (1975–1980)
Religious Affiliation	Catholic/Anglican
Education	Ohio State University, B.A., political science (1974)
Work Experience	Ohio Legislative Service Commission, Researcher (1974–1975)
	Fox News, Host of Heartland (2001–2007)
	Lehman Brothers, Managing Director, (2001–2008)
Political Experience	Administrative Assistant to Senator Buz Lukens (1975–1978)
	Ohio Senator (1978–1983)
	U.S. House of Representatives, Ohio (1983–2001)
	House Armed Services Committee
	House Budget Committee
	Created Balanced Budget Act of 1997
Other Experience	
Relevant Publications	*Courage is Contagious* (1998)
	Stand for Something: The Battle for America's Soul (2006)
	Every Other Monday (2011)
	Other publications

Sources: *www.johnkasich.com, www.wikipedia.com*

JOHN KASICH	Recap of Issues
Economy	Kasich Action Plan: In first 100 days will send Congress a comprehensive plan with a Balanced Budget Amendment
	Return the federal gas tax to the states: retain small amount to support national priorities
	End Washington's micromanagement of education
	Consolidate more than 100 government programs into 4 key block grants and give money back to states
	Consolidate job training and allow it to be administered by the states: allows greater flexibility to train for skills available in those states
	Impose one-year freeze on new regulations: require Congress to have cost-benefit analysis with every new regulation
	Establish strong oversight for all new regulations
	Create third party review capabilities for government agencies appeals processes
	Establish two-year deadline for major infrastructure permits
	Achieve energy independence: approve proposals such as the Keystone Pipeline; allow states to control fracking regulation; repeal regulations that are counter-productive and extreme such as the Clean Power Plan
	Encourage research into effective and conservation friendly technologies

Continued

OVERVIEW OF CANDIDATES 187

JOHN KASICH	Recap of Issues
Taxes	Reduce tax code to 3 brackets: Top rate should be reduced to 28 percent Increase Earned Income Tax Credit by 10 percent Cut long term capital gains tax rate to 15 percent Eliminate death tax; preserve deductions for charitable donations and mortgage interest Cut corporate tax rate to 25 percent Double research and development tax credit for corporations under $20 million Create territorial system that only taxes U.S. produced income Top to bottom review of tax code
Immigration	
National Defense/ Foreign Policy/ Terrorism	Reform International Trade Commission and other bodies to expedite complaints from companies that are negatively impacted by unfair trade practices Renew Navy Create new tools and technologies to protect U.S. in cyberspace "Destroy ISIS-Cannot afford to wait for outcome of 2016 elections to act. Go to Article 5 of NATO. All NATO members would assist France as they work to protect themselves and root out ISIS. Work with the French. Work with them on logistics. Build an international coalition in addition to NATO. Include regional partners Jordanians and Saudis. Make sure Kurds are very well armed. Can't keep waiting. Need to do boots on ground as part of international coalition." *Fox News*, (11-15-15)
Entitlements	Allow states to run Medicaid programs Repeal Obamacare; return control of health market regulation to the states; focus on patient centered primary care
Social Issues	Second Amendment: strong supporter of Second Amendment; protect concealed carry laws Abortion: pro-life; no taxpayer funding of Planned Parenthood

George Pataki Summary Chart

GEORGE PATAKI	Background
	Born 1945
Marital Status and Children	Libby Rowland (1973–present)
	4 children
Religious Affiliation	Roman Catholic
Education	Yale University, B.A. (1967)
	Columbia Law School, J.D. (1970)
Work Experience	Plunkett & Jaffe, Partner
	Chadbourne & Parke, Partner (Post-Governorship)
Political Experience	Governor of NY (1995–2007)
	NY State Senator (1992)
	NY State Assembly (1984)
	Mayor of Peekskill, NY (1981)
Other Experience	Created the Governor George E. Pataki Leadership and Learning Center
Relevant Publications	*Pataki: An Autobiography* (1998)

Sources: www.georgepataki.com, www.wikipedia.com

OVERVIEW OF CANDIDATES 189

GEORGE PATAKI	Recap of Issues
Economy	
Taxes	12% manufacturing tax rate (www.ontheissues.org) Raise taxes on fat cat hedge fund managers. (www.ontheissues.org) Sep 2015) Keep home mortgage deduction and charitable deductions (www.ontheissues.org) Sep 2015 Throw out incomprehensible tax code (www.ontheissues.org) May 2015
Immigration	Deport only criminal aliens; end sanctuary cities (www.ontheissues.org) Sep 2015 Birthright citizenship is OK: don't deport the kids (www.ontheissue.org) Sep 2015 Practical policy: legal residency after 200 hours of service (www.ontheissues.org)-Jul 2015 Immigrants come to work, not for government handouts (www.ontheissues.org) May 2015 No executive orders on immigration (www.ontheissues.org) Jan 2015

Continued

GEORGE PATAKI	Recap of Issues
National Security/ Foreign Policy/ Terrorism	Consider U.S. combat troops to destroy ISIS (www.ontheissues.org) May 2015
	Make sure Iran never has a nuclear weapon (www.ontheissues.org) May 2015
	Risking American lives is necessary to destroy ISIS (www.ontheissues.org) Aug 2015
	Radical Islam poses threat here in America (www.ontheissues.com) Sep 2015
	Give the Israelis massive MOPS bombs to use against Iran (www.ontheissues.com) Sep 2015
	Halt Syrian refugees traveling to the U.S. from Europe: end ISIS' recruitment on social media
	Impossible to vet Syrian refugees: even just one who is a terrorist can threaten us; destroy their training camps; we are at a greater risk for attack than ever before (Interview with Trish Regan on Fox Business News, 11/17/2015)
	Reauthorize the Patriot Act
	What Does George Pataki Believe? Where the candidate stands on 10 issues (pbs.org) May 2015
Entitlements	Would have rejected Medicaid expansion for New York (www.ontheissues.org) Aug 2015
	Obamacare is the worst law of my lifetime (www.ontheissues.org) May 2015
Social Issues	Pro-choice but ban abortion after 20 weeks. (www.ontheissues.org) Aug 2015
	Uphold rule of law: fire those who won't perform gay marriages. (www.ontheissue.org) Sep 2015
	Common Core is a horrible idea (www.ontheissues.org) Jun 2015
	Tackle climate change via private and market based initiatives (www.ontheissues.org) Jan 2015

Sources: *www.georgepataki.com, www.wikipedia.com*

Rand Paul Summary Chart

RAND PAUL	Background
	Born 1963
Marital Status and Children	Kelley Ashby (1990–Present) 3 children
Religious Affiliation	Episcopal
Education	Baylor University (1981–1984), no degree Duke University School of Medicine, M.D. (1988), Residency (1993) American Board of Ophthalmology, (1995)
Work Experience	McPeak Vision Center, Ophthalmologist (1993–1998) Graves Gilbert Clinic, Ophthalmologist (1998–2008) Private Practice, Ophthalmologist (2008–2011)
Political Experience	U.S. Senator (2011–Present) Committee on Energy and National Resources Education Committee on Health, Education, Labor and Pensions Committee on Homeland Security Committee on Foreign Relations Committee on Small Businesses
Other Experience	North Carolina Taxpayers Union (1991) Worked on multiple campaigns for his father, Ron Paul
Relevant Publications	*Government Bullies: How Everyday Americans are Being Harassed, Abused and Imprisoned by the Feds* (2012) *The Tea Party Goes to Washington* (2011)

Sources: www.randpaul.com, www.wikipedia.com

RAND PAUL	Recap of Issues
Economy	Audit the Federal Reserve that currently has too much power
	Congress must live under each law it passes
	Congress should have term limits
	Cut spending in all areas and return power to the states
	Enact a Balanced Budget Amendment
	Support development of energy and initiatives such as the Keystone Pipeline
	Reduce the power of administrative agencies through REINS Act: increases accountability and transparency of Federal regulatory process
Taxes	Fair and Flat Tax
	Repeal entire IRS Code and replace with 14.5% tax on both individuals and businesses
Immigration	Develop a legal immigration process
	Secure the border with a fence built within 5 years
	Establish national identification card system for citizens
	"Trust but Verify" amendment
	Provide ability to track holders of student visas, those provided asylum and refugee status
National Security/ Foreign Policy/ Terrorism	Use military force when necessary and if approved by Congress
	Believes in "Peace Through Strength"
	Will protect the right to privacy of all Americans and will end the NSA's ability to collect illegal bulk data
	Support Israel: proposes "Stand with Israel" act to cut off funds given to Palestinian Authority
	End foreign aid to countries that hate America

Continued

RAND PAUL	Recap of Issues
Entitlements	Social Security: Gradual increase in age for Social Security eligibility; incorporate means testing standard
	Repeal Obamacare: apply free market principles to healthcare; medical expenses should be tax deductible; insurance can be bought across state lines
Social Issues	Second Amendment: uphold Bill of Rights and the Second Amendment
	Abortion: pro-life: government should not fund abortions

Sources: *www.randpaul.com, www.wikipedia.com*

Marco Rubio Summary Chart

MARCO RUBIO	Background
	Born 1971
Marital Status and Children	Jeanette Dousdebbes (1998–Present) 4 children
Religious Affiliation	Roman Catholic/Southern Baptist
Education	University of Florida, B.A. Political Science (1993) University of Miami School of Law, J.D. (1996)
Work Experience	Broad and Cassel, Attorney (2004) Florida International University, Adjunct Professor (2008) Private Practice, Attorney (2008)
Political Experience	West Miami, City Commissioner (1998) Florida House of Representatives (2000); Speaker of House (2005) U.S. Senator (2011) Gang of Eight, Immigration Committee on Foreign Relations Select Committee on Intelligence Committee on Commerce, Science, and Transportation
Other Experience	
Relevant Publications	*American Dreams: Restoring Economic Opportunity for Everyone* (2015) *An American Son: A Memoir* (2013)

Sources: www.marcorubio.com, www.wikipedia.com

MARCO RUBIO	Recap of Issues
Economy	Stop online sales tax: prevent taxation of digital goods and services; defend internet freedom
Fight for Balanced Budget Amendment
Push for line-item veto
Ban earmarks permanently
Reduce size of federal government
Oppose Import-Export bank
Reform budget rules to provide taxpayers with the true cost of government
Put a ceiling on amount regulations can cost economy
Taxes	Cut corporate tax rate to 25%: establish territorial tax system to help bring overseas profits back to U.S.; allow corporations to immediately expense new investments
Three individual tax rates: 15%, 25%, 35% for those over $150,000 individual or $300,000 joint; no deductions except charitable contributions and mortgage interest; refundable personal tax credit instead of exemption; eliminate Marriage Penalty and Alternative Minimum Tax; get rid of the Death Tax; provide higher education tax incentives; address tax treatment of health care
Immigration	Deal with border and future immigrants before granting amnesty
Modernize immigration to win global competition for talent
Cut sanctuary cities off from federal funding
Make it clear that local law enforcement has the right to cooperate with federal law enforcement
Increase penalties for illegal immigrants that return to U.S. after being removed—Impose minimums for those who return after being convicted of an aggravated felony or being deported two or more times

Continued

MARCO RUBIO	Recap of Issues
National Security/ Foreign Policy/ Terrorism	Supports TPP
	Extend Section 215 of Patriot Act
	ISIS: expand airstrikes in Syria and Iraq: deploy forward air controllers; embed U.S. special ops at Battalion level; train Syrian rebels; establish safe zones in Syria; develop a plan to oust Bashar al-Assad; provide arms to Sunni tribal and Kurdish forces; prevent ISIS from entrenching in Afghanistan, Libya and Jordan; weaken financial reserves with sanctions and asset freezes; undermine ISIS' ability to exploit oil resources; expose ISIS' war crimes; prevent jihadists from traveling between their homes and the battlefields
	Refugees: Halt admissions of refugees from Syria until they can be "vetted" effectively.
	Iraq: work with Baghdad to increase Sunni inclusion and autonomy for the provinces
	Push back against Iranian influences in Iraq
	Strengthen U.S. Intelligence: detect potential "lone wolf" attacks
	Israel: strengthen U.S.-Israel alliance and revoke the Iran nuclear deal; fight to move U.S. embassy from Tel Aviv to Jerusalem
	Iran: expose Iran's human rights violations
	Ukraine: defend and restore sovereignty
	Russia: protect Europe from Russian aggression; highlight Russia's arms control violations

Continued

MARCO RUBIO	Recap of Issues
Entitlements	Medicare: reform Medicare; transition to a premium-support system
	Social Security: no changes to Social Security for those in or near retirement age; gradually increase age for future retirees to keep up with increasing life expectancy; reduce the growth in benefits for upper-income seniors while strengthening program for low-income seniors
	Exempt those over age 65 from payroll tax
	Abolish the Retirement Earnings Test
	Obamacare: Repeal; shutter Independent Payment Advisor Board whose goal is to ration services for the elderly; strengthen Medicare Advantage
Social Issues	Abortion: stop taxpayer funding of abortions
	Second Amendment rights aren't the problem: address and solve, not stigmatize, mental illness challenges; review violent society issues and address undermining causes
	Marriage: supports traditional marriage

Sources: *www.marcorubio.com, www.wikipedia.com*

Rick Santorum Summary Chart

RICK SANTORUM	Background
	Born 1958
Marital Status and Children	Karen (1990–Present)
	7 children
Religious Affiliation	Roman Catholic
Education	Pennsylvania State University, B.A. with honors, Political Science
	University of Pittsburgh, M.B.A. (1981)
	Dickinson School of Law, J.D. (1986)
Work Experience	Kirkpatrick & Lockhart, Attorney (1986–1990)
	Echolight Studios, Chairman and CEO (2014)
	Private Practice, Attorney
Political Experience	U.S. House of Representatives (1991–1995)
	U.S. Senate (1995–2007)
	Presidential Candidate (2012)
Other Experience	
Relevant Publications	*American Patriots: Answering the Call to Freedom* (2012)
	It Takes a Family (2005)
	Blue Collar Conservatives: Recommitting to an America That Works (2014)
	Bella's Gift: How One Little Girl Transformed our Family and Inspired a Nation (2015)

Sources: *www.ricksantorum.com, www.wikipedia.com*

OVERVIEW OF CANDIDATES 199

RICK SANTORUM	Recap of Issues
Economy	Pass Balanced Budget amendment: submit plan that balances the budget within 5 years
	Limit federal spending to 18% of GDP
	Audit Federal Reserve
	Increase minimum wage by $0.50 per year for three years
	Approve initiatives similar to Keystone Pipeline
	Block grant highway funds to the states except as necessary for national highways and interstates
	Create Spend-o-meter that publicizes costs of spending agreements (www.ontheissues.org) May 2015
Taxes	Provide corporations with a 100% income exemption for 2 years to jumpstart economy; afterwards a 20% flat tax
	20/20 Flat Tax Plan: 20% flat tax on all individual income; $2,750 per person credit; retention of the Child Care Credit
	No death tax, no marriage penalty, or Alternative Minimum Tax
	Eliminate all tax deductions except charitable contributions and home mortgage interest deduction to be capped at $25,000
	No Value Added Tax
	Restructure IRS
	Zero tolerance for taxpayer abuse

Continued

RICK SANTORUM	Recap of Issues
Immigration	Enforce the law
	Implement a biometric tracking for everyone who has a visa
	Withhold funds from sanctuary cities
	End executive amnesty that has caused border surge
	End automatic citizenship for children born here to illegal immigrants
	Build a wall to seal border with Mexico
	Reduce legal immigration by 25% to preserve jobs for Americans
National Security, Foreign Policy, Terrorism	Faithful advocate of Israel
	Sanctions should be imposed on Iran
	No nuclear deal
Entitlements	Introduce work requirements for means-tested entitlement programs, including federal food stamps program
	Cut means tested entitlements by 10% across the board; freeze for four years and block grant them to the States; States are in a better position to effectively and efficiently manage Medicaid, housing, job training and other social services
	Reform and strengthen Medicare and Social Security
	Fully repeal Obamacare
Social Issues	Education: end federal interference in local education decision (especially Common Core, Race to the Top and No Child Left Behind)
	Marriage: supports traditional marriage and has fought against efforts to redefine marriage; "I would never attend a same sex wedding". (www.ontheissues.org) May 2015-Abortion: outlaw partial birth abortion

Sources: www.ricksantorum.com, www.wikipedia.com

Donald Trump Summary Chart

DONALD TRUMP	Background
	Born 1946
Marital Status and Children	Melania Knauss (2005–Present)
	Marla Maples (1993–1996)
	Ivana Zeinickova (1987–1992)
	5 children
	7 grandchildren
Religion	Presbyterian
Education	University of Pennsylvania, Wharton School of Business, B.S., Economics (1968)
Work Experience	The Trump Organization, Chairman and President (1971–Present)
	TV Personality, *The Apprentice*
Political Experience	Contributor and Fundraiser for Republican Party (2014)
	Sarasota Republican Party, Statesman of the Year (2012, 2015)
Relevant Publications	*The Art of the Deal* (2004)
	Time to Get Tough: Make America Great Again (2015)
	Crippled America (2015)
	Trump for President: Why We Need a Leader, Not a Politician (2015)
	Numerous additional publications

Sources: www.donaldtrump.com, www.wikipedia.com

DONALD TRUMP	Recap of Issues
Economy	We owe $19 trillion and we need a businessman to bring us back (www.ontheissues.org) Sep 2015
Taxes	No income tax for single households earning less than $25,000 and married households earning less than $50,000 (73 million households)
	4 tax brackets: 0%, 10%, 20%, 25%
	Maintain charitable and mortgage interest deductions
	Eliminate marriage penalty, death tax and Alternative Minimum Tax
	One page form for 42 million households
	Personal Exemption Phase Out
	15% tax rate for corporations
	One time repatriation of corporate cash held overseas at 10%
	End deferral of taxes held abroad

Continued

DONALD TRUMP	Recap of Issues
Immigration	Build a wall across Southern border: make Mexico pay for the wall
	Nationwide E-Verify
	Triple the number of ICE Enforcement immigration law officers
	Mandatory return of all criminal aliens
	Defund sanctuary cities
	Detention of illegal aliens until they can be sent home
	Complete visa tracking system: penalties for overstaying visa
	End birthright citizenship
	Control admission of new low-earning workers
	Requirement to hire American workers first: petitions for workers must go to unemployment office rather than USCIS
	Applicants for entry to U.S. must certify they can pay for housing, healthcare, and other needs before entry
	Terminate J-1 visa jobs program for foreign youth: replace with resume bank of inner city youth
	Pause before granting new green cards: force employers to hire from a domestic pool of unemployed and native workers
National defense/ Foreign policy/ Terrorism	China
	Declare China to be a currency manipulator
	Make it uphold intellectual property laws
	Bolster U.S. presence in South China Sea
	ISIS
	Defeat ISIS and stop Islamic terrorists (www.ontheissues.org) Jan 2015)
	National Defense
	Our nuclear arsenal is 30 years old (www.ontheissues.org) Jun 2015

Continued

DONALD TRUMP	Recap of Issues
Entitlements	Obamacare is a catastrophe that must be repealed and replaced (www.ontheissues.org) Jun 2015
	Don't cut Medicare: grow the economy so we can afford the benefits (www.ontheissues.org) Jun 2015
Social Issues	Abortion: I have evolved on the abortion issue just like Ronald Reagan did. I am now pro-life. Ban late abortions except for rape, incest, health (www.onthissues.org) Aug 2015
	Political correctness is the country's problem, not my problem (www.ontheissues.org) Aug 2015
	Education: Common core is a disaster. Cut the Education department way down. (www.ontheissues.org) Jun 2015
	Climate change is a hoax (www.ontheissues.org) Jun 2015

Sources: www.donaldtrump.com, www.wikipedia.com